SOUND SENSE IN SUBURBAN ARCHITECTURE LENT

Publisher's Note

The book descriptions we ask book-sellers to display prominently warn that this is an historic book with numerous typos or missing text; it is not indexed or illustrated.

The book was created using optical character recognition software. The software is 99 percent accurate if the book is in good condition. However, we do understand that even one percent can be an annoying number of typos! And sometimes all or part of a page may be missing from our copy of the book. Or the paper may be so discolored from age that it is difficult to read. We apologize and gratefully acknowledge Google's assistance.

After we re-typeset and design a book, the page numbers change so the old index and table of contents no longer work. Therefore, we often re-move them; otherwise, please ignore them.

We carefully proof read any book that will sell enough copies to pay the proof reader; unfortunately, most don't. So instead we try to let customers download a free copy of the original typo-free book. Simply enter the bar-code number from the back cover of the paperback in the Free Book form at www.RareBooksClub.com. You may also qualify for a free trial membership in our book club to download up to four books for free. Simply enter the barcode number from the back cover onto the membership form on our home page. The book club entitles you to select from more than a million books at no additional charge. Simply enter the title or subject onto the search form to find the books.

If you have any questions, could you please be so kind as to consult our Fre-quently Asked Questions page at www. RareBooksClub.com/faqs.cfm? You are also welcome to contact us there. General Books LLC™, Memphis, USA, 2012.

꙳ ꙳ ꙳ ꙳ ꙳ ꙳ ꙳ ꙳

IN
SUBURBAN
ARCHITECTURE
CONTAINING
Hints, Suggestions, And Bits Of Practi-cal
Information For The Building Of Inex-pensive
COUNTRY HOUSES
BY
FRANK T. LENT, M. S., Architect
Author of "Sensible Suburban Resi-dences"
With Illustrations by the Author
SECOND EDITION—REVISED
New York
W. T. COMSTOCK
1895

After an experience of twelve years, largely filled up with the designing and superintending some two hundred sub-urban residences in different parts of the United States, it seems tome that a straightforward, brief, and practical lit-tle book on the subject of inexpensive Country Houses will be of great service to those who are about to build. This is but a collection of bits of practical in-struction which an architect has gath-ered during years of practice, and which has been, of great use to his clients.

The Preface above was written two years ago, for the first edition. The au-thor is pleased to state that the results have been far beyond his expecta-tions—many scores of people have tes-tified as to the book's usefulness.

Frank T. Lent. Cranford, N. J.,
May 1, 1895.

COPYRIGHT, 1805, BY
Frank T. Lent.

Sound Sense in Suburban Architec-ture AND
Sensible Suburban Residences.

Each with many Illustrations. Each 1oo pp., 8vo, Cloth.

By FRANK T. LENT, Architect, CRAN-FORD, N. J.

Books full of Hints, Suggestions, and Bits of Practical Information for the economical building of inexpensive Country Houses. Drawings from Actual Houses. Worth many times the cost to anyone intending to build.

Published by W. T. COMSTOCK, 23 Warren St., New York.

Sent Post-paid to any Address for $1. 00 Each. Very Valuable and Practical Books.

EXTRACTS FROM REVIEWS.

"This very pretty work contains very good suggestions for cottage residences, illustrated by drawings from buildings erected. There is no question that many excellent hints can be found for those contemplating building."—*Scientific American.* "Frank T. Lent, an architect of twelve years' experience, has pub-lished a book of practical bearing, re-lating to most questions connected with the erection of suburban residences. His bits of advice are reliable and sugges-tive, and he has enforced them by a number of illustrations of his own."—*Review of Reviews.* "This interesting tome contains hints, suggestions, and bits of practical information for the building of inexpensive country houses. It will certainly be of great benefit to those about to build. It enters into the numerous details of house-building that are so perplexing to the novice, and will save the prospective homeowner not only money but worry. It is commended to our readers." —*Commercial Adver-tiser, Detroit.*

"It is profusely illustrated with many plates of elevations and ground plans and its suggestions are terse and well chosen. One of its novel features is the addition of a set of specifications with practical notes and comments."—*N. Y. Advertiser.*

"The suburban house might be called the American specialty, for the Amer-ican's country house is usually only a suburban house standing apart. The houses in Mr. Lent's book are better than the average in such books, and his hints and suggestions are sound as his title page claims."—*The Nation.* "' Sound Sense in Suburban Architecture ' is the title of a prettily bound book published by Frank T. Lent. It contains many illustrations and is a book full of hints, suggestions, and bits of practical information for the economical builder. It is worth many times its cost to those contemplating building. Mr. Lent has had over twelve years' experience and has designed and superintended over two hundred houses in different part of the United States."—*Art Interchange.*

"Curiously enough, the title of Frank T. Lent's ' Sound Sense in Suburban Architecture' is not a misnomer. He talks about houses as one having experience; shows drawings of a few which are not frights, and discusses points of construction and equipment in a common-sense way. Mr. Lent is entitled to public gratitude in that he does not undertake more than he can perform, or talk 'any-manhis-own-architect" nonsense. Architects are as necessary as doctors and lawyers, and houses without their services will continue to be, as in past, sick and sorry specimens."—*N. Y. Recorder.*

"This beautiful little volume is from the pen of an architect whois well known as an authority on this particular subject, and whose original plans, drawings, and illustrations give added value to the text. Mr. Lent's suggestions, so admirably presented, are most timely; for this is the age of suburban life, and the problem of cottage building and furnishing is one of paramount importance. The author disposes of the question of site and construction, and then goes on with the problems of furnishing and exterior improvements, treating all topics in a masterly way that shows his perfect familiarity with the subject. The book will be worth many times its weight in gold to any person interested in the construction of a modern suburban residence."—*Blue and Gray.*

"Mr. Lent's volume is full of practical suggestions. Not many plans are offered, but such as appear are good, and none of them are affrighting in point of expense. There is more text and also-more attention to interior details, than is usually found in volumes made for the thousands who are hoping to make homes in villages. The drawings are effective and show clearly to persons of taste who consult this book the difference between the ideas of a mere builder and the man who has studied architecture with a view of harmony and to making the most of such opportunities as space may grant. Much of the author's work consists of a set of specifications which is offered as a guide and model, and which should be of great use." —John Habberton *in Godey's.*

"A handsome volume of one hundred pages beautifully bound, well printed and elaborately illustrated on fine heavy paper.

"The work is both practical, artistic, and suggestive, and the country architect as well as his city brother will find in it much matter of interest that will be new to him however unwilling he may be to confess the fact. The builder will find the practical pointers in this work an invaluable aid in his profession. In his preface the author says:

"' It seems to me that a straightforward, brief, and practical little book on the subject of inexpensive country houses will be of great service to those who are about to build. This is but a collection of bits of practical instruction which an architect has gathered during years of practice, and which has been of great use to his clients."

"The author is entirely too modest in his claim, for the book is really much more than a collection of bits of information. It contains suggestions and studies which will be found instructive and interesting to the architect and student of architecture as well as to the general reader."—*Architectural Monthly,* "We have before us about the neatest and most useful book on suburban architecture we have ever seen. It is a little volume of about one hundred pages, beautifully printed, and has on the title page the name of Frank T. Lent of Cranford, N. J., as the author. That Mr. Lent is an architect of skill and taste there is evidence in his book to prove. He takes up and discusses the general subject of suburban architecture, how to adapt the house to the situation and all to one's circumstances. After giving some pretty examples of houses erected by him, Mr. Lent goes into the details of light, ventilation, drainage, water, and all those seemingly little things, the absence of which interferes with the comforts of a home, however beautiful and costly it may otherwise be, and it is in these practical elements that the reader will find the greatest charm in the book. If all the details of house building in this little volume are carefully studied and followed out, absolute satisfaction is sure to be the result. We most cordially recommend it to every man contemplating building now or in the future."—*Newark Times, N. J.*

"The author of this book, who has been engaged for the past twelve years principally in designing and superintending country houses, writes from the knowledge and experience thus gained, and gives in a brief and straightforward manner such hints, suggestions, and practical information as maybe useful to those who contemplate building inexpensive country houses. He grasps the situation intelligently at the start, and, as a basis of all house building, presents the indisputable fact that the house must be a home, and that the only way that success can be gained is by a conscientious study of the needs and customs of the family and their individual habits, and then plan the house to meet these requirements. This is not so easily done, as the client or his family may be far from settled as to what their desires really are, but always, of course, within a certain financial limit. To get the most for the outlay in comfort, space, and style is the desire and dominant feeling of every home builder. To have the house large enough to accommodate the family, but with no waste room; to have a modish exterior without the sacrifice of interior comfort or convenience; to spend a limited amount wisely on decoration or ornament, always allowing a generous sum for the best approved sanitary appliances, are the great questions that ought to be considered by every man who builds a home for himself, or by those who build for the real estate market.

"It has been said that a wise man never builds, but buys a house, and so profits by the mistakes of others, but this need not hold true if the architect is alive to the needs of his client and the client duly considers the most important points, and is not led away by an errant fancy which is attracted by the 'pretty things' which a graceful prospectus often shows. To avoid such things and gain the greatest advantage from given space, situation, and materials brings out the worth and talent of the architect, and the title of this book earns its name of 'Sound Sense' in that it advocates and demonstrates these and all principles which should govern everyone who builds a home. The author has added sketches and plans of houses of his own design, some interior views, stables, etc. The subject of drainage is well considered, with directions for sewer ventilation, cesspools, etc. There is a chapter on water supply and heating, and the specifications for mason and carpentery work, plumbing, heating, and lighting are well defined and considered. Although the author does not put his work forward to be followed or copied, it can be commended for its honesty of purpose and be recommended as a help to prospective builders."—*Architecture and Building.* HOUSE FOR J. V. BAMCER, CRANFORD, N. J.

SUBURBAN ARCHITECTURE.

I.

But all men are concerned with architecture, and have at some time of their lives serious business with it.—Ruskin. TO the mind of the hard-worked American of the present time "there is no place like home"; nor is there to be found an expression of more comfort and delight than the word *home* conveys when one may apply it to his own house. No other kind of property is as well worth striving for. The ownership of property of other kinds may give enjoyment, but whatever amount and variety of possessions may have been secured, the real pleasure we find in them is not to be compared with our enjoyment in the ownership of a home.

We are told that Jenny Lind was the perfect picture of noblest womanhood. Her artistic career was quite Napoleonic in its splendid and unbroken success. In fact hers was the conquest of Europe, yet she gladly exchanged all her triumphs for the simple happiness of home. She sang "Home, Sweet Home," not only with the grandest artistic success, but also with the deep feeling and tenderness which could-only arise from a loving personal apprehension of the charming significance that lies in this dear old word. The sweeping universal interest in it makes the thought of its meaning of deep value to everyone. Be it a simple, unpretentious cottage, a modern residence, or an elaborate country seat, it means the same charming thing to its owners, in whatever class or station of life they may be. Yet of the thousands who yearly reach that period in their lives where they have, for the first time, both the means and desire to possess a home for their very own, there are many who do not know anything of practical use as to how to proceed, how to formulate their ideas—and, above all, how to get full value for the often hard-earned funds they wish to invest.

"Shelter from the inclemency of the weather," says Violet le Due, "is the first step in architecture." And that was the idea of our early colonists, who had first to protect themselves from the rain and wind, the cold of winter and the heat of summer. But in these days more than this is demanded. The house must be well heated in cold weather, and properly ventilated; must have the best possible sanitary conditions, and, above all, must be artistic as well as well constructed. But even the early colonists of this country, who had to be satisfied with the more primitive ideas of houses for residence, soon began to build in that graceful and charming style which to-day we return to with keen and sharpened appetite.

The term "Colonial" implies a structure that is substantial, picturesque to all Americans, and historic in its associations.

"We realize the beauty of our own colonial architecture," writes a clever architect. It is our own. The Colonial is all we have, and every day we find that a yearning for the good old style is becoming more and more general.

It is said that all European architecture is derived from Greece, through Rome, and the history of architecture is nothing but tracing the various modes and directions of this derivation.

Our Colonial is derived from the same source. The clew is easily followed back to a point of origin, and there is something very much more satisfactory in an art that had its beginning in a venerable classic integrity than in new-fangled and short-lived novelties.

"Classical art has been assailed repeatedly," we read in Vignola, "and these attacks have not been answered with DE WITT HOUSE, CRANFORD, N. J. anything like the vigor of spirit in which they were made, because the faithful followers of that art have felt secure in their position, and have replied most forcibly by continuing in its practice."

Of what earthly use and how unsatisfying are all these pretentious, but ridiculous, styles—as they are called—which are springing up in the majority of our suburban towns? We are indebted for the origin of the most of them to the stupidity and thoughtlessness of ingenious (?) designers who have never honestly studied architecture ten hours of their lives—designers who know not the meaning of good composition, good color, *ensemble,* and picturesqueness.

"All very good," say the people who are ready to secure a home, "but how are we to insure success in obtaining what we desire?"

In order to proceed intelligently it is necessary to become somewhat posted in suburban architecture—and it is believed that a careful study of the plans, specifications, and notes herein given will put one on the right road. Not that the buildings represented by the drawings are intended to be set up as acmes of perfection, nor that they are to be followed as models, but are suggestive of important practical ideas. If they graphically explain and illustrate the hints herein given their design will be accomplished. If a young couple have any individuality of character, and the average amount of common sense, they will not put up with a pattern house or a duplicate of a neighbor's, on the same principle that there is no real, lasting pleasure in the possession of a chromo, no matter how cleverly or handsomely framed, but of which duplicates may be so easily obtained. Duplication or repetition soon renders any object common and distasteful.

The people who resort to patent medicines when their child is ill often make a fatal mistake. It is much more *sound sense* to send for a doctor, if there is a good one to be had. It is a disadvantage that good professional services in designing suburban houses of small cost often cannot be secured. When, however, the services of a good architect are within reach the owner cannot make a mistake in securing them. This advice is so generally recognized that it is not necessary to argue the case here. It is true that the majority of well-posted architects are *too* busy with more important and more profitable work to pay attention to small houses. Yet there have been painted as many small pictures which are as full of interest, of artistic effect, and of careful design, as large ones. Why should not we have as good design, as good color, and as good sense in our small homes?

The quaint interest of the cottages and some of the large houses of European towns unquestionably arises from the fact that each was built to suit requirements and tastes of the owner, and a remarkable fact is that many of them are of very low cost as well as in good taste.

People have already begun to study for themselves, to become intelligent on the subject of suburban and domestic architecture, and already improvement is noticeable.

The chances are *against* your finding a pattern or patent house planned to suit you. You may think it will answer your purpose, until you get into it, when you will find you have made a sad mistake. The idea that there is a fashion to follow in houses is as ridiculous and as short-lived as fashions usually are. Fashions change rapidly, and your ideal house soon becomes stale, and old, and behind the times.

The only way to get a house thoroughly satisfactory is to study closely the habits, customs, and needs of the family that is to occupy it, and then plan the house to suit. This can only be done by hard, conscientious study.

In adapting the designs of a modern house to special requirements it is of course a difficult matter to adhere in all respects to the pure, straightforward Colonial style of architecture. But whatever departure in minor details may be required in accommodation to our later mode of life or personal conveniences, the old Colonial grace, simplicity, and refinement are sure to make a favorable impression in contradistinction to foolish attempts at outward display, bedaubing with scroll-sawed brackets, freaks of the wood turner's fancy, fantastic color, lop-sided design, and cheap, senseless ornaments.

The shape, color, and form of a house defines very clearly the character, education, and taste of its owners; and the general arrangement, interior decoration, and selection of furniture show at once the social condition and the standard of refinement of the inmates.

THE NOBLES HOUSE, ATLANTIC HIGHLANDS, N. J.

The cut above shows a residence on similar lines to that on page I, with the stone chimney omitted and considerable porch and balcony space added, so as to make it more desirable for seashore and summer use. The actual estimates for this house aggregated less than thirty-five hundred dollars, including complete mason, carpenter, painter, plumber, and furnace work. The plans show staircase-hall, drawing room, library, dining room, butler's pantry, and kitchen on first story; five bedrooms and bath, second story; and four bedrooms in attic. Construction comprises sanitary plumbing, creosote stained shingles, hard pine floors, fine cellar with laundry, range, two open fireplaces, and servants' closet.

The beautiful is sometimes more useful than the useful.

—Ruskin. IN designing a house it is as well to bear in mind one or 1 two principles, and, as far as possible, to carry them out. The strongest work which is to-day done in designing is the simplest, and those designs which have required the greatest amount of study are often the ones which appear the simplest.

In good architecture utility and beauty go hand in hand, and neither need be sacrificed to the other. As the house is planned the mind should be continually turned from that which is useful to that which is beautiful; or if the inclination is to produce picturesque effect, it is important to remember that no house would make a desirable habitation if its usefulness should be sacrificed to its prettiness.

No ornamental feature or work should be put on a building unless it has a reason for being there, either as useful or as indispensable to good construction. What is meant by truth 7 in architecture is just this, the adaption of ornament to some practical purpose, so that everyone shall see that it is the right thing in the right place.

There is one practical rule which should never be departed from in arranging the plans for a dwelling. It is that the living side of the house, that is, the side which is principally inhabited, should face the south rather than any other point of the compass. The more sunlight there is in a house the smaller the doctor's bills will be, to say nothing of the cheerfulness and pleasure the sunlight brings with it.

THE HALL.

Probably no room in the suburban house is more important than the hall—the room which is too often treated as a mere runway to get to the other parts of the domicile. The impression first formed of the building—at least as far as the interior goes—is the most lasting one, and will be carried by visitors as they go around through the other apartments.

The first impression should therefore be an exceedingly pleasing one, and the arrangement nowadays generally adopted is to make the hall a reception, sitting, and staircase room all in one. Add to this a good-sized fireplace with mantel, a comfortable spacious seat or couch, and as the result of this the hall becomes an exceedingly interesting place to pass the time in, and one with which the visitor cannot help being pleased at first sight, especially if the color is well handled. Now the hall does not come under the head of a living room, and usually has to occupy the northerly and most undesirable side of the house. There may be no sunlight to cheer and brighten it up, and consequently the right thing must be done with the walls and windows. The former may be treated with decorations of warm, cheerful yellow hues, while the windows are the places for stained glass, which fortunately can be had in these times in very good designs for very reasonable prices.

In furnishing, there is but little required for the hall; an old-fashioned chair or two and a table should be selected, if of oak all the better. Put down a rug of good color, and the effectiveness of the room will be accomplished.

In order to avoid the ungainly and unpopular hat rack it *is* very desirable to provide a closet for hats and coats in some convenient place, and, if possible, go a step further and put a lavatory in this closet.

If, on account of expense, there is but little hard wood to be used in the house use that little in the stairs and mantels; and if there is to be but one hard wood floor have it in the hall in preference to any other place.

It is a good idea, when possible, to arrange it so as to separate in some manner the staircase part from the hall proper by means of a beam along the ceiling, the same supported by columns at each end. If there is a good place for a nook, or for a couch on which one can rest in front of the fire, it always adds to the picture the element of repose and comfort, which cannot be gotten out of a sofa or lounge.

The drawing room or parlor is used much more now than it ever has been; that is, it is not kept shut to be opened only on the arrival of guests or for airing. The drawing room of to-day, in most country houses, is used for a music room, general sitting room, and often for a library. There is something honest and above board in seeing the family use the house as if they had no fear of spoiling the rooms and furniture. It shows a good breeding and training to use the best in the house without injury or defacement. One must naturally feel awkward and out of place in other people's parlors if not allowed the free occupation of his own. The drawing room should be the largest in the first story; it should have a fireplace and the most important mantel, and should be separated from the hall and other rooms by commodious doors sliding out of sight when opened. In decorative management it is well that this room be of a color scheme contrasting strongly with that of the hall. There is nothing more beautiful than the white and gold, though a much darker coloring may be pleasant if it has the sunlight, which should by all means be secured for it if possible.

THE DINING ROOM.

The dining room should get the morning sun. A pleasant, cheerful breakfast goes a long way in making one goodnatured for all day. The evening meal occurs after sunset for the greater part of the year. This room should be longer, if possible, than it is wide, so that the table may be extended without filling the room full.

A bay window, where plants may be kept in winter, is always pleasing; and a closet for fine china and glass is very useful.

People go to the dining room to appease their appetites, and it might be a good plan to have the decorations and fur nishings very simple, rather than so luxurious as to distract the attention from the purposes for which the room is built.

The dining room may better be without a fireplace than any other room in the house, because, unless the room is of great size, someone's back will be roasted. A recess for the sideboard is a very pretty feature, and has its usefulness too, for it is not necessary for the sideboard to project out into the room and be in the way; but if this is not feasible the sideboard may be located in the bay, under a stained glass window. One of the prettiest arrangements of color for a dining room is what is called the Whistler effect—a treatment in yellow and white for the walls, natural pine trim or woodwork, and an oak table, sideboard, and chairs.

J The Butler's Pantry.

While the dining room should be near the kitchen, it is always well to separate the two by means of a good-sized closet—commonly called the butler's pantry. This should be well supplied with cupboards with glass doors, lockers, and butler's sink, where the china and glass can be washed and dried instead of taking it to the kitchen. You say, "We shall not have a butler." Very good; the very people who cannot afford the butler are those for whom every convenience should be studied, and the pantry as described is one of the most useful contrivances in the whole house. The doors between this pantry and both the dining room and kitchen should be hung to swing both ways, and also to be self-closing. By means of these the smells of cookery are confined to the kitchen—the place where they belong—because in passing between the two rooms it will be impossible to have both doors open at the same time. These self-acting doors admit of the passage of a person with both hands full, as they are easily pushed open with the knee or shoulder, and a tray can be carried right through both doors without stopping to open or close them.

THE KITCHEN.

The kitchen, first of all, should be well supplied with closets. "A place for everything and everything in its place" was never more applicable than right here. There should be a large sink and ample drip board, good places for tables, plenty of light, and good ventilation. The kitchen generally occupies the north side of the house; and this should be so, for in the summer it should be as cool as possible, and in the winter it is always warm enough. A good kitchen is a great assistance in getting and keeping a good servant. It should be cheerful—

paint the walls and ceiling a bright straw color.

Piazzas.

Piazzas—the most useful part of the house in the summer, and worse than useless in the winter, because they keep off sun when it is most needed—troublesome things to manage, these. You cannot have them around the living side of your house; they can only be put on the northerly and perhaps the westerly sides. A very good method is to build them out and projecting away from the house, far enough to be spacious, and yet to not take up too much room on the sides of the house. A very bad method is to project them under the second story where air cannot circulate freely. Sometimes piazzas are built without roofs, an awning being put up in the summer time to keep off the hot sun, and taken down in the fall in order that the sun shall have free access. This device is very commendable.

AWNING AND BAY. THE DEN.

The majority of people living in suburban towns have but a small collection of books, which can be disposed of in a bookcase or two, and as these cases may be placed in any room, there is but little use for a library; but there is good use for a den—a man's own room, to which he can retire with his friends and have some privacy. These rooms are becoming more and more popular; they are found in nearly all of the larger houses. As many persons do not like to have the entire house fumigated, they are especially useful as smoking rooms, and are generally furnished with a comfortable couch or lounge, and are often made extremely interesting with a decoration of arms, armor, antlers, and other accompaniments and recollections of various sports and games. If the den can have an exterior side or rear door opening into the garden, or perhaps toward the stable, the man of the house will find it very convenient, and if a small conservatory could be arranged to fit on the den a great deal of pleasure and satisfaction might be derived from its products and garden-like appearance during the cold and dreary months of winter.

THE SECOND STORY.

A careful arrangement of the rooms in the first story will generally give good rooms on the second, and the partitions should be kept over each other as far as possible. The bedroom principally used should have a fireplace. Each bedroom should have a good-sized closet, and spaces should CONSERVATORY. be provided for the bed, dressing case, and any other large pieces of furniture. From the second-story hall there should open closets for linen and bedding, and a small closet fitted up with shelves for medicines. The stairs to the attic should be open—nothing makes one think that the attic is uninviting and garret-like so much as a closed and narrow stair. The attic rooms should be made as interesting as possible, and the entire attic should be lathed and plastered. The open stairway will be a great aid in ventilating in the summer time.

A STABLE.

A stable is an important adjunct to a country house if one can keep a horse, and in every case stables should be of the same general design as the house.

Stables.

It is common belief that a *port'e cocltire* is a purely ornamental and very useless feature to the country house; but this is wrong. A well-arranged *porte cochh-e* is very useful; in fact it is quite difficult to get along without it when one thinks how many times during the year it is necessary to embark or disembark in vehicles when the rain is pouring down in torrents.

THE CELLAR.

A cellar may be developed into a very useful part of the house. There should be a small room with a window in it quite near the foot of the cellar stairs, and this fitted up with shelves for a cold room. The coal bins should have partitions carried up to the ceiling so that the coal dust cannot get all over the cellar when the coal is put in. Another room might be developed into a laundry, another into a carpenter's shop, etc., etc. At completion let it all be whitewashed and you will find that you will have something to show your friends even down cellar.

III. DRAINAGE. THERE are two sides to

the drainage or sanitary subject: the inside and the outside—and each is equally important.

The sewage must be gotten safely out of the house, and after it is out it must be safely disposed of by cesspools or sewers. There is no poetry in this. The disagreeable business of plumbing must be accomplished in a safe and sure manner, because carelessness and ignorance may mean death.

The Inside.

To be comfortable and meet the demands of the day the modern suburban home must be fitted up with a bath room containing bath, basin, and water closet (it is far better, when practicable, to have the water closet in a small apartment adjacent to and separate from the bath Bath Room. room). There must be also kitchen sink, butler's sink, and laundry wash trays—to say nothing of a water closet for servants' use. This list may be reduced or several other fixtures may be added, but the kitchen sink, the bath, and water closet are indispensable, and they must be so arranged and connected as to be absolutely safe against conducting or generating that dread demon *sewer gas.*

The first requirement is that all of the plumbing pipes must be thoroughly gas and water-tight.

They must be fitted up so as to have a thorough flush (by flush is meant a quick flowing, as a jet or stream of water thrown suddenly for cleansing or washing purposes), and should be well ventilated. The waste pipes inside the house should be of heavy cast iron or lead, according to what they have to carry off—the main line soil pipe 4", and the wastes from basin, bath tub, sinks, and wash trays not less than 2". No earthen pipe should be used inside, and the waste pipes should be fitted at convenient places with appliances so that they can be easily inspected and cleaned out.

It is very easy to see that a line of waste pipe from any fixture to the sewer—or cesspool—without traps would be an open duct for bringing gas directly and continually back to the house, and perhaps into the very center of the house.

The only method known for preventing the return to the house of injurious sewage gases—either from sewer or cesspools—is the use of traps. These are really bends in the pipe arranged so as to hold liquids, these liquids making a continuous seal or obstacle, which prevents the gases from passing back through the waste pipe when empty— and they *are* empty more than nine-tenths of the time.

But traps are not continual and perfect seals, and have to be fitted themselves with appliances to make them safe.

The worst enemy traps have is siphonage. Suppose, by way of explanation, that a volume of water is suddenly started on its journey down the main soil line—as when the water closet is flushed. That this volume of rushing water with its attendant atmospheric pressure will draw or siphon the smaller quantity of water out of the traps is easily understood; and, of course, if the traps are empty the sewer gas not only can come directly through the waste pipes, but is actually invited and conducted to the house.

To make traps invulnerable against siphonage was devised the system of back-airing or ventilation, viz.: providing each trap at its crown or on the sewer side of the seal with a pipe running directly to the open air above the roof of the house, these back-air or vent pipes counteracting the siphonage, and the water in the traps remaining undisturbed. The vent pipes must be of large size and of short runs, however, or they will not do their work, and the scheme of ventilating or backairing the traps becomes, in large plumbing systems, quite complicated, and in small houses is expensive.

A comparatively new device has been in use for some years back, is highly commendable, and is used in place of the vent pipe to a great extent. It is the McClellan Anti-Siphon Trap Vent, and when placed on plain traps will prevent siphonage and save expense. Then there are skillfully devised traps which are made to be un-siphonable, the Sanitas

family. It is not advisable to discard the ventilation of the main soil line under any circumstances, and, being a 4" pipe, it may be depended upon to ventilate the trap of the water closet safely and surely. In a word, then, good plumbing in the house consists mainly of keeping the sewer gas out by means of the seal of traps, and having these seals so protected as to be constant and unimpaired under all conditions.

The Outside.

In selecting a suburban town in which to build one would do well to locate in one where there is a good sewer system; the cesspool difficulty would not have to be considered, and the continual expense of emptying and cleaning would not have to be met. But if the cesspool has to be used let the greatest care be exercised that every precaution is taken to have it as safe as possible.

As the soil pipe passes the walls of the house, just outside of the wall, there should be a 4" running trap fitted with a 4" vent pipe of cast iron from its crown, and the vent pipe carried up to the ground directly over the trap; and at a point one foot above the ground the vent pipe should be provided SECTION OF VENT AND WALL.

with ventilating cap. The work just described, and outside of the house walls, is usually done with earthenware traps, vent, etc., which are very good, but a cast iron trap and vent are far better, and if the work is well done the owner may feel certain that the main bulk of virulent gas will never reach the inside of the house.

But aside from this ventilation it is very important that the deadly gas should be prevented, if possible, from coming so near the house. To accomplish this the device of ventilating the cesspool itself should be adopted. A cesspool should not be nearer than fifty feet, and should be ventilated through its top.

The vent is indispensable, because a closed cesspool, when partially filled with the sewage and excrement from the house, is nothing more nor less than a retort in which foul air and dangerous gases are formed. When, by fermenta-

tion and chemical action, these gases accumulate sufficient force by expansion they will force their way back to the house through the drain pipes. The vent at the cesspool allows escape to the fresh air, which soon renders the gases harmless. The ventilation of the cesspool is often accomplished by ventilating the soil pipe at the house, and carrying the vent pipe up to the roof. This is not considered desirable because of the easy access the free and noxious gas has to the windows of sleeping rooms. Carbonic acid gas is largely the principal ingredient of cesspool and sewer gases, and being heavier than air it naturally falls as soon as liberated. This being the case, if it is liberated close to the ground and a few rods away it is rendered harmless by the fresh air before it can reach the house.

It is also common to have two cesspools, one connected with the other by a pipe, so that the liquid sewage can pass to the second cesspool, and from it can be pumped out for the purpose of fertilizing the garden.

The laying of the drain pipe should be watched very carefully. A good grade of salt glazed vitrified pipe should be used, 4" in diameter inside, and the joints should be made per fectly tight with cement mortar. Four inches is the proper size for drain pipe connecting the ground with the sewer or cesspool; neither more nor less. If the pipe is smaller than 4" it is very liable to clog up, and if it is larger than 4" the ordinary flush of the fixtures in the house is hardly sufficient to clean the pipe thoroughly.

The underground pipes connected with the conductors for carrying off the rain water from the roof should be separate lines, and run with a perfectly even grade to some lower ground, or the street gutter. The rain water cannot well be taken to the cesspool, because it would soon fill the vault full. It is sometimes considered desirable to run one line of conductors from the roof to the sewer drain, if this drain be connected with a regular sewer. This is done for the purpose of thoroughly flushing out the pipe whenever there is a heavy rain. NOTE: Besides the ventilation of the drain pipe *outside* of trap (as per cut on page 21), the system of soil and vent pipes should be supplied with a fresh-air inlet in basement and inside of trap seal so as to provide an ample and continuous circulation of fresh air throughout the entire system.

It will be noticed that the selection or use of elaborate fixtures is not mentioned in the foregoing pages. The owner can go to one of the score of shops, which exist in any large city, and select fixtures to fit his purse without any difficulty. It is common practice among plumbers to put up a fine array of plated and complicated fixtures and thus please the eye with the finishings, while the sanitary methods used are of the rankest and most inadequate character. This should be avoided. Get the SYSTEM right first and then, if there is enough money left, go in for fine fixtures.

IV.

VVATER SUPPLY AND HEAT.

UBURBAN houses derive their supply of water from wells, k—' cisterns, or springs. It is a very rare occurrence that a real good spring is available, with cisterns we are familiar.

The commonest source for a water supply is the well, and provided it is a properly constructed well, there is but little doubt of its furnishing the best kind of water to be had. Probably more sickness arises from the use of impure water than from the use of impure air or any other cause. Surface water is almost always contaminated in some manner, and the keeping clear and free from it is the point to be sought after in all wells. It is almost impossible to keep surface water from finding its way into an open well.

If one goes down deep enough, and constructs the well so that no surface or other foul water can get to it, there is hardly any question but that the water will be very nearly chemically pure. The best wells are what are called driven wells, and are commonly constructed by driving a wrought iron tube (pipe) from 2" up to 4" in diameter into the ground until the water is reached. The pipe or tube may be spliced as fast as it is driven down by means of couplings, and the lower end may be fitted with a

point perforated with numerous holes. The pump is attached to the upper end. These wells, of course, cannot be put down successfully if large masses of hard rock are encountered, but it is very common to overcome the obstacle of rock and bowlder either by drilling or by the use of dynamite. In order to keep the surface water out of the well it is a common practice to drive down a larger tube or casing for a distance of from fifteen to thirty feet, and run the main well tube through this casing.

An interesting story is told by a New Jersey welldriver which is valuable by reason of its practical points. He was required to sink a well in a place where the surface soil was of gravel, and in which there was no difficulty for the first twelve feet, but at this point a bowlder was encountered which turned the tubing out of its course. Several locations were chosen a few feet away, and about the same obstructions of bowlders or large cobbles were met with, until it was found almost impossible to put down the well anywhere near the desirable position. The first location was returned to, and a 2" tube sunk until the bowlder was again reached. A drill was worked for a few inches more, and small dynamite cartridges dropped into the tube. After several shots the bowlder was sufficiently shattered so that the tube could be sunk some little distance, and this method was pursued until the bowlder was entirely passed. The tube was then driven through several feet of gravel and sand, and finally struck hard and solidly upon a strata or bed of rock. The casing was cleaned out, and a drill as large as could be accommodated by the casing was inserted, and the well actually drilled through from 4' of hard rock, and then through successive layers of softer shell and rock. This well was carried down in the manner described to the depth of 77', which was 6' below where water was first found in good quantities. The drill was replaced by the tubing, and after the casing had been thoroughly settled into the first bed of rock, thus insuring perfect protection against surface water, the tubing was connected with a pump, and an unfail-

ing supply of absolutely pure water secured.

HEATING.

Of the various methods of heating the suburban dwelling by long odds the most common is furnace heating. With a good, tight, warm-air furnace of liberal size, with commodious, well-made conducting pipes, and with a well-arranged cold air duct, there is but little danger of furnace heating being detrimental to health, especially if the house is pro vided with fireplaces which act as outlets for foul air, and thus aid in ventilation and circulation. The furnace chosen should be one with heavy castings, tight joints, ample size, and it should of course be located as near the center of the house as possible, so that the hot air flues may be near by. If the furnace is too small you may depend upon it that it will be necessary to overheat it in cold weather, thus burning the oxygen out of the air, and filling the house full of dead instead of fresh air.

For effective heating steam heat must be given a place, or, heating by means of hot water; these two methods are usually considered too expensive to be used except in more valuable and expensive houses, but there is no better or more economical way of heating a suburban residence. With a tubular boiler of wrought iron, such as the Gorton, there is no danger, no difficulty in handling (in fact it is quite automatic), and a great saving in the coal bill. A great many expert heating engineers prefer, with good reason, heating boilers of cast iron, such as those made by the American Boiler Co.

If direct radiation is used the Perfection Radiators are the most artistic and best constructed in the market.

The most delightful fire that one could possibly have is of hard wood in an open fire-place, provided the house be also well heated by other methods. There is nothing more charming on a cold day than a roaring wood fire in a properly built fire-place. It is true that half of the heat goes up the chimney, but then the best of ventilation is secured and the loss and gain quite balance each other. It is not judicious to depend upon fire-places for heat in severe weather. There should be other and adequate means of heating auxiliary to the fire-places; fire-places really only heat one side of everything or every person in the room.

V.

THE DRAWINGS. THE drawings used for the illustrations in these pages are not experimental in any sense of the word. Houses have in each case been built from them, and have given thoroughly good satisfaction. The drawings and sketches referred to as Set No. I were made for the residence of John W. Banker, Esq., which was built at Cranford, N. J.; those referred to in Set No. 2 are almost identical with the residence of Dr. John C. Van Dyke at New Brunswick, N. J.; and Set No. 3 represent the De Witt house on Cranford Avenue, Cranford, N. J., now being built. The drawings followed herein are not published for the purpose of offering them as model houses, or for "selling the plans." In fact the owners would object seriously to the houses being duplicated.

If the reader by means of these can get a few hints or suggestions which may be applied to any house, the illustrations will have done their work.

The Banker house, the most old-fashioned of the lot, is shingled from top to bottom. The shingles were dipped before being applied in creosote shingle stain of brownish gray colors on the walls, and moss green on the roof; the cornices and exterior trim are painted Asbestos paint ivory white; the Roman columns are of Georgia pine, which, with the interior trim, are finished in natural wood with varnish. The stonework is of the roughest random rubble. The stones are gray, and many of them covered with moss and lichens. The mortar used for pointing is black. As far as practical use goes, the plans are quite perfect, and yet the rooms are divided and arranged so as to produce very pleasing pictures and vistas.

House No. 2 is clapboarded one story and the balance shingled, the clapboards being painted, and the shingles stained rich brownish red colors, such as may

be found on an old copper kettle, and the trim is dark brown. The foundation and chimneys of red brick laid in black mortar harmonize very nicely.

As this house is located on the bluffs overlooking the Raritan River it was necessary to extend the porch considerably. This house was built and completed ready for occupancy, including the architect's fees, within the sum of five thousand dollars.

Set No. 3 was designed especially to meet the requirements of a family of four or five persons, keeping within the sum of three thousand dollars, and giving a thoroughly comfortable, well-built, and pleasant home. Of course the hall is not as much developed as those in the other drawings, but the house includes everything absolutely necessary for convenience and enjoyment. The color treatment is as follows: second story, gables and roof shingles silver gray; cornices, trim, and clapboards very light lemon yellow; blinds *verd antique* green; columns natural Georgia pine; brickwork and chimneys light red brick laid in yellow mortar.

The house in the frontispiece is a delightfully simple and quiet example of Colonial, both exterior and interior. The Otis house is one of stone, very imposing, and built at a cost of thirty thousand dollars. The Pastorius houses are two very much admired residences on Cascade Avenue, Colorado Springs, Col. The house for F. C. Moore (page 42) is an example of a commodious summer residence, where an expenditure of ten thousand dollars is necessary and desirable. Strength, solidity, and repose are its characteristics. The residence of Mrs. Bates at Cranford has just been completed at a cost of eight thousand dollars, and is a very commodious house of Colonial arrangement with some twenty large rooms.

VI. SPECIFICATIONS. IN order to build intelligently it is necessary to have good plans and specifications, even though you do not have the services of an architect in superintending the construction. The drawings, if complete and thoughtfully made, are, with a little study, easily understood by anyone, but the spec-

ifications, which, by the way, are quite as important as the drawings, generally receive but little attention, investigation, or study.

A set of specifications require very close study in order that every point of construction be clearly understood by the owner and the artisans. To accomplish this the meaning of the many technical terms should be made clear to the owner. Now while the methods prescribed for accomplishing various results may be perfectly clear to artisans and mechanics, they may be Greek to the uninitiated owner, and with these facts in view it has been thought desirable to insert herein a regular working set of specifications with notes and explanations so arranged as to be easily followed. The specifications used for this purpose of general illustration, would, with a very few changes, answer for the perfect and complete construction of either of the dwellings herein illustrated, or for any ordinary frame house. With a clear understanding of these specifications it would not be a difficult matter for the owner to work up a set for himself which would be sufficiently thorough and complete for the construction of a substantial frame house, even though the plans and drawings which were to be followed were very rough and incomplete. It may take hard 41 study to reach this point of "clear understanding," and the owner must not think it a short task, to attain that knowledge which the architect has acquired only by years of faithful study.

Throughout the following specifications will be found places where additions, omissions, or alterations will be necessary, and in a number of instances several different methods have been described where only one will be required. The idea is that the owner, if he is working out a set for his own use, may choose whichever he desires and omit the others. By putting all the information in there is not so much chance of anything being omitted.

The specifications proper occupy the tops of the following pages, with notes and comments below, so that they may be easily compared.

'!»-. RESIDENCE F. C. MOORE, ESQ., NAVESINK HIGHLANDS, N. J.

SPECIFICATIONS

Of Labor and Materials for a Frame Dwelling House to be built for from the drawings hereto attached at The building to be built on lot situated on

The work to be constructed and completed in every part in a substantial and thorough manner according to the accompanying drawings, to the full extent and meaning of the same, and to the approval and acceptance of the owner or superintendent.

The contractor or sub-contractors are to provide all material and labor necessary for the complete execution of everything described or noted, including transportation, scaffolding, apparatus, and utensils needed for the same.

All materials to be the best of their respective kinds, and the workmanship to be first class.

It is very common to find in the specifications at this point the words "or reasonably implied." In case of dispute this really means nothing; it is much better to have the specifications, etc., complete and accurate, for contractors can only be held to do those things which are clearly mentioned. The owner's name, location of site, town, and state should be inserted in the vacant spaces above. The vacant spaces throughout the specifications are intended to be filled out by the owner when the exact class of material or labor is settled upon, as it is often the case that materials commonly found in one locality are quite unknown in another. By talking with contractors or with those who have already built it is an easy matter to find out what kinds of materials are commonly used in any locality for the various parts of construction, and if one wishes to keep down the expense of his house he will be exercising sound sense by following along the usual road, and selecting materials and methods which are familiar to the workmen rather than insist upon things new and strange to them.

The Detail and Working drawings to be used in connection with the plans and elevations show all dimensions of the work. Follow the dimensions on the drawings rather than measure by scale.

All written notes and figures on the drawings are to be considered and followed as a part of the drawings and specifications.

The contractor must carefully and thoroughly protect from injury all of the finished work, during the erection and completion of the building, and especially, must give attention to the thorough protection of the floors during plastering, covering same carefully with

It is almost impossible to define clearly with words many things which are capable of an easy, graphic explanation and definition; consequently it is common for architects to resort to the placing of notes, figures, and signs on the drawings for delineations or explanations of the work. It should be carefully explained to the contractors that they shall carry out their instructions as to care of finished work to the letter. It is not a difficult matter to get a contractor to protect his work, but it is very troublesome to get one to replace slightly damaged work. This is of special importance in the matter of floors. It is so common now to dispense with carpets and use rugs that hardly a house is built without some finished floors. It is best, of course, to line those floors which are intended to be finished; that is, lay a rough hemlock floor diagonally on the joists, and put down the top flooring after plastering; but it is so often necessary to keep down the expense that this is not feasible. A dozen barrels of dry sawdust scattered evenly over new floors will protect them very nicely against the stains of mortar, lime, etc. , during the plastering, and is far better than building paper, which is soon torn or worn through. It is well to insert in the specifications "protect floors during plastering with sawdust."

Specifications And Drawings.—The specifications and drawings are intended to co-operate, so that if any work or material is described by the specifications, and not shown on the drawings, or, *vice versa,* if anything is shown on the drawings and not mentioned by the specifications, the same is to be executed by the contractor or contractors as if shown or described by both specifications and drawings.

Drawings.—The following is a list of drawings which accompany these specifications:

Front Elevation, Two Side Elevations, Rear Elevations, Section and Sheets of Details, Foundation Plan, First Story Plan, Second Story Plan, Attic, and Roof Plan.

This is to forestall the event of the contractor coming to the owner and saying, that so and so is not mentioned in the specifications, while it is a point which is clearly described in the drawings.

When the contract is drawn, and at the time of signing, it is very important that the owner should then and there deliver to the contractor a complete set of drawings and specifications. Then there can be no afterclaps—no chance for the contractor to accuse anyone with having meddled with or changed either after the contract was signed, or say that such and such a drawing was handed to him afterward. If necessary to make any changes, be sure that these are carefully stated before the execution of the contract. (For further information in regard to contracts see special chapter on same.)

There are two methods of letting out the contracts for the construction of dwellings. The owner may let the entire work to one contractor—generally the carpenter—who will sublet the minor contracts, or the owner-may make separate contracts for each department of the work, viz.: Masonry, Carpentry, Painting, Plumbing, Heating, etc. The, specifications above, are written to cover the one contract method.

MASON WORK. EXCAVATION.—Excavate for the cellar as shown by the foundation plan, besides 6" all around, to depth sufficient to give full 7' ceiling height between the top of finished cellar (concrete) floor and the under side of the first story joist. Excavate trenches for footing courses 2' o" wide, and an average of 8" deep below cellar excavation. Excavate trenches under all walls, cellar partitions, chimney foundations, and cellar piers as shown. Also excavate for cistern, cesspools, and drain pipe as shown or specified.

Feet are generally described by the sign '; inches "; thus: 7' 6" (7 ft. 6 in.). Floor timbers are usually called joists.

The 6" all around referred to above is done in order to prevent the mason from laying the wall up against the bank— a very easy and a very slovenly way of doing it—if the excavation is the exact size of the wall. This additional excavation of 6" is also for the purposes of allowing the mortar in the walls to dry, of giving the workmen room enough to do the plastering thoroughly on the outside of the wall below grade, and of giving the owner a chance to see, with his own eyes, how the work is done.

The trenches for footing courses should be graded from 6" deep to 10" deep (an average of 8") and toward the lowest corner of the lot, so that same can be well drained; and the object of projecting them beyond the walls on either side is to secure a more substantial and solid footing. The interior and other trenches are not put in so much on account of drainage as for securing strong foundations to carry weight. These footers being the same under all walls the latter will naturally settle evenly, and not more easily in one place than another.

In making the excavation keep the good top soil separate from gravel, etc., and when notified by owner fill in and pack against the cellar walls and grade up to the bottom of underpinning, sloping off ground on all sides of the building, and remove, if required, any surplus dirt and rubbish. In grading put back the top soil on the top of the gravel or common dirt.

The separation of the rich soil from the common and unenriched earth below is a matter of no expense, and admits of the same being replaced on top of the common earth all ready for lawn making. This item saves a great many dollars, but is often not put in the specifications at all, in which case the contractor throws out the earth helter-skelter, and when the grading is completed it is found that considerable expense is

necessary to get the ground fit for planting grass seed. One might also have the good soil removed for a distance of several yards around the excavation. The elevations should show clearly the line of the natural ground and the line of the proposed grade. An exact understanding should be arrived at between the owner and the contractor as to who shall furnish water for mason's mortar, who shall furnish fuel, stoves, etc., in case the plastering is to be done in cold weather, and when and to what extent the contractor is to clean up the house at completion. These are often sources of dispute between the parties to the contract, and it is much easier to settle them at the beginning than at the ending.

The depth to which the excavation shall be carried must be decided by the general location. First, do not get the bottom of the cellar below the bottom of the sewer or below the line of standing water, otherwise it will always be damp. Second, do not get the house too near the ground when graded, or too high above it—there is always a happy medium between the squatty and the gawky.

CESSPOOL: *Excavation:* Locate the cesspool 50' o" from the building and where shown on the foundation plan. Cesspool to be dug out 10' o" deep, and 8' o" in diameter.

Wall up the cesspool with 12" stone, laid without mortar, to a point within 5' o" of ground. Spring a brick arched top over same, with a 20" manhole. Carry the manhole up to the ground—or grade line—and cover the same over with a 3" flagstone. Lay the brick with cement mortar, and provide a 4" cast iron vent pipe from the crown near the manhole. The vent pipe to project above the ground 1' o", and to be capped with a ventilating cap.

The dimensions above prescribed are, of course, optional. If these are thought either too large or too small they may be easily changed to suit. If thought desirable the stone wall can be laid in mortar also. The manhole admits of cleaning out the cesspool easily, and the flag cover prevents anyone from falling in. Ventilation could be accomplished by having a hole drilled into the flagstone,

but the vent pipe is better, because no dirt, rain, nor animals can get in. The vent pipe is for the purpose of providing any gas which may have been formed in the cesspool with an easy access to the open air; because sewer gas once free in the open air soon becomes diluted, weakened, and rendered practically harmless. If a second cesspool is desired it should be mentioned above; also the position of same, location, length, and size of connecting pipe, and also if the cesspool is to be made water-tight. (See cut, page 22.)

No arrangements are made herein for the construction of a privy or its vault. If there is to be a stable on the premises, or any other outhouse, the privy might be attached thereto, but unless it can be concealed in some manner it is an unsightly object, and had better be done away with.

Drain AND Sewer Pipe: Dig trenches not less than 3'o' deep where shown on the foundation plan for the drain and sewer pipe, and grade carefully. The trench for the sewer or pipe to the cesspool to have a fall of *1"* to 1'. Put down first-class salt glazed vitrified drain pipe of dimensions as marked, laying same carefully and making all joints perfectly tight with cement mortar. The sewer pipe to have a 4" running trap just outside of house wall, same to be fitted with a vent from the crown, and said vent carried with cast iron pipe to a point 1' o" above ground, where cap with ventilating cap. Each conductor from the roof to be connected with the drain pipe with a cast iron pipe.

The use of cast iron pipe (see cut, page 21) in connecting conductors with drains saves a lot of trouble and expense, as the tile pipe, where it comes to the ground, is easily affected by frost, and the conductor pipe of either tin or galvanized iron is fragile, and easily broken or bent out of shape. The vent pipe is put in the crown of the trap so as to prevent siphonage, and thus secure a constant seal, extending from drain pipe below ground up to a point, 1' o" above ground, the object being to allow sewer gas to escape outside of the house walls rather than force its way through the trap, which it would probably do if there was no vent. The exact location of the cesspool or entrance to the sewer should be shown on the foundation plan, and all of the runs of the drain, sewer, or rain water pipes which are to go below ground. This plan may be kept for future reference, and some time may serve a good purpose in assisting the owner in locating any pipe, and thus save the trouble of digging up the entire lawn.

CISTERN: The excavation for the cistern will be 8'o" in diameter, and 8' o" in depth. The bottom of the cistern will be built of three courses of good, hard burned brick laid in cement mortar. The bottom will cover the entire size of the excavation. On this bottom start the walls; same to be 12" walls to the height of 4' o", and the same material as specified for the bottom.

Build the brick dome 8" in thickness from the top of the side walls, join the same into a 20" manhole; manhole to be covered with 3" flag, and to be built up to the grade line. The walls of the cistern are to be thoroughly plastered, on the outside as well as inside, at least a $y2''$ thick, excepting on the bottom, where put down a full inch all of cement plaster.

Use F. O. Norton's Rosendale cement and clean, sharp sand in the proportion of three of sand to one of cement, excepting for the plastering, which may be of equal parts of sand and cement.

Furnish the cistern with a 4" cast iron ventilating pipe carried from the dome up through the ground, and at a point 1' o" above the ground cap the same with ventilating cap. Put in a 2" overflow pipe, carrying same to lower ground or to some drain other than the cesspool or the sewer.

If it is to be a filtering cistern it will be necessary to build a brick wall 8" across through the center, with several 4" openings at the bottom, and two short walls about 20" from the center wall, and parallel to it; these short walls to be 18" high for the reception of filtering material, which is usually carefully cleaned gravel and washed charcoal put in each filter box in alternate layers.

(See cut, page 24.)

Some masons cannot seem to do anything without Portland cement, and if the mason is set upon it, it may be better to allow him to use it, though the Rosendale above specified is excellent material.

FOOTING COURSES: Fill all trenches prepared for same with small stone well rammed in. These may be coarse cracked stone, or small field stone, and on these lay a heavy coat of cement mortar; whole 2' o" in width. The top of this footing course will be level with the bottom of the cellar concrete.

In putting in drains, sewers, etc., owner can connect at lowest portion of these footers, which are also drains, and thus drain thoroughly under all walls. It must be borne in mind that the trenches for these footing courses are graded with considerable pitch in order to carry the water to the lowest corner of the building (see note, page 46).

The object in making the footing course also act as a drain is obvious. This course projects 6" on the outside of all walls, consequently any surface or other water following down the walls must go into these drains, which are graded so as to carry it off, when it might otherwise accumulate and force its way up into the cellar. This contrivance of itself is often the means of securing a dry cellar. It should also be noticed that the top footing course is on a line with the *bottom* of the cellar concrete, so that when the drains are full of water the water line would be below the cellar concrete.

If the ground at the bottom of cellar excavation is found to be soft, sandy, or in any way unstable it will be necessary to put down the footing courses of solid concrete, made by mixing cement, gravel, and sand with the small stone; and in case this has to be done it is well to provide drainage around house by means of drain pipe laid with open joints so that the water can easily enter.

FOUNDATION: *Stonework:* To be a first-class random job of good hard stone, well laid in F. O. Norton's Rosendale cement mortar. Plaster outside of same

below grade carefully and neatly, and yz'' thick. To be at least 16" walls, and all exposed underpinning to be of selected field stone, pointed in black mortar made of "Peerless" Mortar Color.

The stone must be well bonded together, tied in, and all joints well filled with mortar. Care must be taken with the exposed portions so as to produce an artistic effect, and at the same time secure substantial walls.

No more sensible foundation could be put under a country house than one of stone, if there is a stone mason about who knows his business. The most select quarry and cut stone cannot produce as pleasing an effect as one of common weather-marked field stone with their varying grays, moss greens, and soft browns, but they must be well put together, and it is rare to find a stone mason with enough artistic sense and ingenuity to do the work properly.

If such a mason is not available it is better to take the above paragraph out of the specifications and substitute this:

Foundations: To be of brick as per following instructions, all to be 12" wall, well bonded in every sixth course, and laid in Rosendale cement mortar. Plaster outside of same below grade carefully and neatly $l/2''$ thick. All exposed underpinning to be laid in black mortar made of "Peerless" Mortar Color.

Care must be taken in selecting a good brand of cement. F. O. Norton's Hydraulic Cement cannot be too highly recommended (F. O. Norton Cement Co., 92 Broadway, New York), and the "Peerless" Mortar Color made by S. H. French & Co., Philadelphia, can always be depended upon.

BRICKWORK: All brick to be a first-class hard, burned brick of manufacture. Lay same wet in warm weather, but if laid in cold weather the brick must be dry. Only thorough and first-class workmanship will be allowed.

Porch piers to go at least 3' o" below ground, and to porch sills above ground. Plant these on good footers of small stone as shown, and cap each with 3" flag size of pier. Build and carry up chimneys as shown by drawings. These may be laid in mortar properly made of clean sharp sand and lime, up to the topping out above roof, where use black mortar of cement as before mentioned, and selected brick of even and dark color.

Good bricklayers are to be had in every small town in the United States. If the owner is careful in the selection of his brick, cement, lime, and sand, and watches the progress of the work with ordinary vigilance, there should be no difficulty in getting a first-class job of brickwork in every case. When the brick manufacturer is settled upon the blank in the specifications may be filled out. Great care should be taken that the brick laid below the level of the ground are laid in cement mortar, and the wall carefully plastered on the outside. When it comes to the chimneys or piers in the cellar lime mortar will do just as well. It is very important that the brickwork in chimney shall be very carefully done, and no spaces or holes left anywhere.

It is very common to plaster the exposed brickwork both on the foundations and chimneys, but this is a very bad practice, and should not be resorted to. Honesty is the best policy. A good dark brick neatly laid in black mortar is much more honest than veneering with paint, which, by the way, will have to be replaced every year or two, and thus increase the cost of maintenance. Nothing is in worse taste than so-called "stucco" walls laid out in blocks and painted to imitate cut stonework.

Build all flues very smooth on inside, and leave clean at completion. Mason will be held responsible for working of each flue and fireplace, and required to make good same; each must have a separate flue. Plaster the outside of all chimneys where same is hidden by lath and plaster. Each fireplace opening to have a J" X 3" iron. Put in earthen thimbles and galvanized iron stoppers where required. Build furnace flue separate from all others. Insert for furnace flue an 8" thimble, same to be at least 8" below ceiling; also build in furnace flue a 5" thimble in cellar for laundry flue, if required. Turn trimmer arches for all hearths. After the flues have been drawn

into shape and size as shown on second story plan put in terra cotta flue linings for each, and carry each separate to top of chimney. These linings to be of sizes as shown, and to begin at a point 3' o" below ceiling of first story, and these linings to be inclosed with 4" exterior wall of brick, and same to be built in thoroughly and *solid with* brick and mortar all the way.

The extra precaution of plastering chimneys and flues on the outside behind lath and plaster often saves trouble and disaster arising from fire, and when the terra cotta flue linings ARCH SECTION THROUGH FIRE PLACE AND TRIMMER ARCH.

are used danger from fire is reduced to an absolute minimum. These terra cotta flue linings can be had at but very little additional expense, and there is no place where additional expense is as desirable as here. ASH Pits: Carry up the chimney walls in cellar as shown to form ash pits, drawing in at the top so as to inclose pits in brickwork. These to have 12" X 16" iron doors with frame in cellar; build these in during construction. Fit the fireplaces with automatic ash-dump grate. Build up with concrete the entire hearths (over the trimmer arches) to within 2" of top of finish floor. Line each fireplace with fire brick 4" on back and sides, same laid in fire clay mortar, and as per detail. Build in these fire brick during construction.

The ash pits herein referred to are built in the foundations of the chimneys, as shown by the drawings, and the automatic dump grates in each fireplace on the first floor admit of the ashes and dust passing directly to the ash pit; when the ash pit is filled the iron door above referred to will allow the ashes to be removed by way of the cellar. These little contrivances are of great service to the housekeeper, because the ashes from fireplaces do not have to be taken up and carried out over the carpets of the principal rooms in the house.

By lining the fireplaces with fire brick as above specified the best possible construction is secured, far better than the use of the thin cast iron linings which are commonly resorted to, be-

cause of the superior ability of the fire brick to withstand heat. The fire brick can be had in any color, and when neatly laid present a very satisfactory appearance. The fire brick linings also hold the heat, and throw it long after the fire is out.

If the iron linings are preferred the fire brick can be omitted. Wm. H. Jackson & Co. of New York make a very beautiful line of linings, grates, and other iron and brass work connected with the fireplace, and their linings are extra heavy. The Jackson Heat Saving and Ventilating Grates are the best where a continuous grate fire is required for actual heating purposes. E. A. Jackson & Bro., New York.

Range will be portable and furnished by owner. No setting necessary. The range will have a hearth projecting 12" in front of same, and of the width of range. The hearth to be of

This specification does not include the furnishing of tile for facings or hearths. These will be furnished by owner, and set by contractor. The facings will be of 6" tile, and the hearths of 3" tile. Build in kitchen chimney a flue for ventilating over the range, same to have an 8"X 10" register.

Portable ranges are now used almost altogether in country houses. The absence of brick jambs saves a great deal of kitchen space, and the portable range is of much easier access than those that are built in. Then, too, there is considerable expense saved, as no heavy brickwork nor stone lintels are necessary. The portable range can be fitted with a projecting hood which will collect the fumes and smoke of cookery. There should be a small flue in the kitchen chimney opening above the range and under the hood, which flue will carry off the smoke and fumes. It is not absolutely necessary to have brickwork under the portable range, as there is no danger from fire, but some people prefer it.

The hearth may be of smooth slate, or, what is far better, of glazed tile. The tile is much neater, more easily taken care of, and does not become saturated with grease. By specifying that the owner shall furnish the tile for facings for fireplaces and for the hearths the selection of the tile is left entirely in his hands, and he is not at the mercy of the contractor's taste. The artistic tile industry in this country is so far advanced that there is no difficulty in getting very beautiful tile at but little expense.

The American Encaustic Tiling Co. of 140 West Twentythird Street, New York, make very artistic tile for facings and hearths.

The owner can purchase direct of them or of their agents.

Stone sills of 3" flag projecting 2" beyond wall for all cellar windows. Steps of hatchway to cellar to be of 3" flag; also same to have brick risers, and to project into hatchway walls at least 4". All hatchway masonry to be laid in cement mortar, and to be absolutely secure against dampness and moisture. The top step and coping to be of flagstone, as above specified. Furnish the piers in cellar and under piazzas and porches with caps of flagstones, these to be of the size of piers 3" thick. Each chimney is to have a cap of flagstone neatly perforated for each flue. Flag not less than 3" thick.

Stone chimney to be built of same stone as that used for foundation, and same may be built as large on the outside as mason considers desirable, but shall have not less than 12" walls. Special attention must be paid to the batter, otherwise chimney will present a top-heavy appearance.

Flag walk of first-class 3" flagstone to be put down as shown or where marked on plan. Bed thoroughly in gravel, cinder, or sand, and trim edges neatly at completion.

The sills as specified above are rough and not fine cut or tooled work. If considered desirable the cutting should be added to the specifications. The idea of furnishing all the brick piers with stone caps is for the purpose of giving the timbers a secure bearing, instead of allowing them to cut their way down into the brickwork. Any girders resting on foundation walls of brick should rest upon blocks of stone built in for the purpose.

Should the owner desire not to have

the stone chimney the above clause may be taken out, or may be changed to read for brickwork instead of stone. The exterior chimney is a very pretty feature, and unless it is necessary to cut out on account of expense, the owner will surely be well satisfied in the long run.

If walks of gravel, wood, or cracked stone are desired in place of the flag the change should be made accordingly in the specifications.

Back Lath And Back Plaster: To be put on all of the exterior walls of the house between sill and plate, and between studding. Lathing will be done on furring strips put up by carpenter, and the plastering will consist of a good $1/2"$ coat, of strong brown mortar.

The building is to be beam filled with 4" walls of brick on all exterior walls and interior walls.

It is the air in the 4" space between the exterior sheathing and the interior plastering which really keeps out the cold in winter and the heat in summer. It is hard work to get either cold or heat through a "dead air" space, and, of course, if there are two air spaces it is so much more difficult. Now the object of back plaster is to double the air space, and it consequently makes a house much cooler in summer and much warmer in winter. The expense of back plastering a house is paid in three or four years by the saving in the coal bill.

The air which makes the floors of the first story cold comes in over the top of the foundation and around the sill. The beam filling prevents this, and closes up all of that space between the floor joists from the top of the foundation up to the flooring. To have the floors warm it is better to lath and plaster the ceiling of the cellar as is specified under the head of plastering. The dead air space thus inclosed between the cellar ceiling and the first story floor is far more efficacious than any other method, unless the floors be "deafened," *i. e.,* provided with an inch or two of mineral wool laid on boards at the middle of the joists, which, like back plaster, doubles the dead air space. (U. S. Mineral Wool Co., New York.) BACK PLASTERING.

CONCRETE: Level off cellar bottom, thoroughly settle, and put down 3" of good concrete. This to be three parts clean coarse gravel, and one part (Rosendale) cement. The finish coat to be 1" thick in addition to the above, and to be of equal parts cement and clean, sharp sand, all worked up flush and true, and protected until hard. This to include area or hatchway bottoms. Form a drain all around the exterior walls, same to be graded to the lowest corner of the cellar. Dig out the bottom under the location of furnace of size shown to a depth of 1' 0" below the cellar bottom, and concrete same as above. Pitch off the cellar bottom to the bottom of this furnace pit, and finish all neatly. The wash trays and water closet not to be placed in position until concrete is completed under same.

Many people prefer to use Portland cement for the finishing of the cellar concrete, but a good quality of Rosendale cement, if carefully manipulated, will produce a very hard, smooth cellar floor. F. O. Norton's can be recommended.

A slight depression or trough may be formed in the cement around and near the cellar walls, and this slightly graded to the lowest corner where it may be connected with the drain. If this interior drain or trough is put in, a running trap, with vent pipe as before specified, should be put in so as to prevent any drain or sewer gas from entering the cellar. Over the drain there should be an iron grating, so as to prevent animals from getting into the drain. If, however, the footing courses under the exterior wall are built as before described, there is but little need of interior drainage for the cellar.

The object in lowering the furnace is to get plenty of rise for the conducting pipes. It may not be necessary at all if the runs are short, or perhaps 6" excavation would answer. Great care should be taken with the concreting of the bottom of this pit, and if the ground is at all wet it should be dispensed with.

LATHING: All walls, partitions, ceilings, and all places which are studded or furred are to be lathed with the best pine laths, full size, placed not less than one-quarter nor more than three-eighths of an inch apart, and nailed on every stud with lath nails. All joints must be broken every 18", and all to be placed horizontally. Long vertical joints will not be allowed, nor lath put on vertically, to finish at angles or corners. All lath at corners or angles must be nailed to solid furrings, and lath will not be allowed to run from one room to another behind studding. The lather must call upon the carpenter to furr and straighten all walls, ceilings, etc., and block and spike all studs together solidly at angles. In all cases lath below grounds to floor and behind all wainscoting. In attic rooms and closets will be lathed and plastered. Also the exterior walls of same showing from head of stairs. The entire ceiling of cellar, and the partition walls of servants' water closet, cold room, and laundry to be lathed. Hot air pipes, flues, etc., and a space 10' square over furnace to be lathed with first-class metal lath.

To secure real good plaster walls considerable attention must be given to the lathing, and each point above mentioned should be looked after carefully. If King's or Rock Plaster, or any other prepared plaster, is used for plastering the walls, the lath should be placed on a shade closer than a quarter of an inch apart; but in no case should they be placed closer than an eighth of an inch apart.

The breasts of chimneys should be furred and lathed instead of plastering directly on the brickwork. If part of the wall is plastered on the brick and the balance on lath the brickwork may settle, and make bad cracks. It is often the case that the settling of the chimney differs from that of the house walls. Consequently if the furring strips are fastened securely to the adjoining woodwork, and not to the chimney brickwork, the weighty masonry may settle considerably and yet not carry the walls along with it. Metal lath should be used instead of wood on all studding near furnace flues. The specifications should be made to say exactly how much lath and plastering there will be in attic and cellar.

PLASTERING: The walls and ceilings of all rooms and apartments throughout to be plastered with two good coats ot sand, lime, and hair mortar scratch, and brown coats and (third coat) hard, white finish on all walls and ceilings. Use good unslacked lime of manufacture, goat or cattle hair, and clean, sharp sand free from loam, all to be well mixed and manipulated, and stacked in the rough for at least ten days before applying to the walls. The first coat to be properly applied with sufficient force to secure good clinches. All lime must be worked through a fine mesh wire sieve before being mixed.

Ceiling of cellar throughout to be lathed and to have a good coat of brown mortar. Also rooms in attic.

The walls and ceilings of the first and second stories to be "roughcast" or sand finished for painting. The partition walls of servants' water closet, cold room, and laundry to be plastered.

The specifications above call for ordinary plastering material, but after a test of a number of years some of the patent wall plasters or cements have been found to be of great value, especially King's Windsor Cement. The advantage in using the patented plasters arises from the fact that the ingredients are carefully chosen and thoroughly mixed by machinery with the sand, and in exactly the proper proportion. All there is to do is to add the water, and apply according to the directions, and a very hard, durable, and substantial wall will be the result. Of all the methods of treatment for house walls there is nothing more artistic, substantial, or more sanitary than oil paint applied directly to the roughcast or sandfinished walls in flat tints. While the wall papers of today are very fine, yet there is something about the stereotyped pattern which makes them very tiresome, and when papered walls are compared with these painted walls the sanitary conditions of the latter are far more desirable. Physicians agree that a good hard wall treated with paint is the best, and it is a very pleasant thought for the housekeeper that the walls can be washed and cleaned.

The mason is to run first-class 8" plaster cornices in the rooms of the first story and 6" plaster cornices in the rooms of the second story. These to be according to the details, and in each of the first story rooms above mentioned put up a plaster centerpiece 2' o" in diameter as per detail. The second story rooms having cornices will have a centerpiece 16" in diameter to correspond.

Finally: Mason is to do any and all patching after other mechanics, and leave all his work in first-class shape. He is to leave the house broom clean, and to clean carefully all glass which may have been in any way spattered or soiled with plaster.

It is rather the exception than the rule to put up plaster cornices and centerpieces nowadays, the plain frieze reaching directly to the ceiling being the general custom.

A picture rail, cornice mold, and perhaps chair rail will be found useful; the latter especially is a good thing, as it saves the walls.

A mantel of pressed and molded brick or terra cotta makes a very pretty and substantial mantel for the hall. The materials for any of this class of work, as well as for fire brick linings for fireplaces, and terra cotta flue linings for chimneys, may be had of the Staten Island Terra Cotta Lumber Co., Woodbridge, N. J. The Philadelphia and Boston Face Brick Co. also furnish a beautiful mantel, as well as the Peerless Brick BRICK MANTEL Co., Philadelphia. James Rodgers' House.

CARPENTER'S SPECIFICATIONS.

Carpenter's specifications of labor and materials required for a Frame Dwelling, to be built for according to the plans and drawings hereto attached.

The house to be full balloon frame, put together in the strongest manner; perfectly true and plumb, and in accordance with the framing drawings. The frame and rough sheathing is intended to fill mason work so that the water table will project over face of underpinning.

Studding, 2" X 4"; 16" from centers.
First Story Joists, 2" X 12"; 16" from

centers.

Second Story Joists, 2" X 12"; 16" from centers.

Attic Floor Joists, 2" X 10"; 16" from centers.

Rafters: Main Rafters, 2" X 6"; Shorter Rafters, 2" X 4"; all 16" from centers; Hips, 2" X 8"; Girts, 1" X 6"; Partition Studding, 2" X 4". Door Studs and all opening studs 4" X 4". Hip rafters to be doubled up.

For an ordinary medium size frame dwelling the balloon frame, if carefully put together and well spiked, is amply strong and substantial, and will withstand the action of the wind without any apparent effect. The timber sizes herein mentioned are those commonly used in balloon framing.

The 2" X 4" studding is often supplemented by 3" X 4", and sometimes by 2" X 6", and the floor joists generally used are 2"X 10" instead of 2" X 12", but the stiffness of the floor is one of the most important things to accomplish in the construction of the house. Nothing is more awkward or trying than to see the chandeliers move up and down when a person walks around in the second story or to have the plaster continually cracking off.

Sixteen inches is the proper distance from centers for all timbers, as this will exactly accommodate the laths, which are 4' o" long, and each lath will have four bearings and nailing places. The girts are let into the studding on the inside edges for the support of the second story and attic joists, which joists are notched on the girts.

Plates, 4" X 4"; Posts, 4" X 6"; Sills, 4" X 6".

Girders as shown on plans (for framing, see p. 65).

Bridging, 1" X 4" every 5' o", herring bone, both joists and studding. Cut square ends (see cut.)

Attic ceiling joists, 2" X 4"; 16" from centers.

Porch And Veranda Timbers: Joists, 4" X 10", framed into sills 4' from centers; sills 2" X 10" doubled.

Sub-joists, 2 "X 10"; 16" from centers.

Rafters, 2" X 4"; 16" from centers.

Hip rafters, 4" X 6".

Ceiling of porches to be " X 3" planed, matched, and beaded Southern pine; ceilings on rafters finished with fillet and cove. All other necessary timber required throughout the building to be1 of good, sound hemlock sawn true and die square; free from sap, shakes, dry rot, or other imperfections impairing its strength and durability, and all timbers used throughout must be prepared and framed, according to the plans, sections, and details.

The plates are to be made of 2" X 4", doubled, instead of 4" X 4" solid. It is just as easy to do this, and it is much stronger.

The 4" X 6" sills laid directly on the foundation wall is the ordinary method of construction. A box sill is much better in many respects, and is commonly omitted because of additional expense. The bridging should be cut square at the end instead of on an angle. If well spiked into the joist the square end bridging will bite and hold much better.

While hemlock is here specified for the framing timber, spruce would be much better, and in many sections of the country can be had for the same price. Spruce is a much stiffer material, and is often used for the floor joists and rafters when not used for the whole building. Hem BRIDC/NC M/BK..., r lock is a staple framing material of the country, and when used of the sizes herein specified will be amply strong to carry all the weight which can possibly be put upon it.

Framing: All joists to have the crowning edge placed upward, and properly sized where required. Also prepare and size all studding, etc. The floor joists to be carried on top of the cellar girders, and these girders to be made of 2" joists bolted together with $/&" bolts every 1' 6". All trimmers and headers must be framed double; and in no case allow less than 2" between chimney, brickwork, and timbers. As far as possible, stock moldings, doors, sash, casings, base, etc., may be used. Owner to have choice of patterns for the same. Fur off all chimney breasts and chimney brickwork for lathing; no

plastering to be allowed on brickwork. Fur for back lath between the studs of the exterior walls of the house from sill to plate, with 1" X i%" strips nailed to the studding and against the exterior sheathing, so that the back plastering will come directly in middle of studding.

Gables: Frame all dormers and gables as per drawings. Where shingles are used they are to be plain butts, no fancy shingles.

It is but rare to find a perfectly straight hemlock joist. There is invariably a bend in these sticks, and in placing the joist this bend or "crowning edge" as it is called, should be placed upward. In larger buildings it is common to cut a crowning edge on the beams so that when the floor is loaded and the timbers sag, the floor will yet be perfectly level.

There is a large variety of stock moldings to be had in almost every town, and from them a selection can always be made which will answer the purpose nearly as well as if special moldings were designed at a much greater expense. If back plastering is not to be put in, the sentence above relating to the furring for the same may be erased. It is seen by the above that the use of fancy and ornamental shingles is emphatically prohibited; not that these shingles should be thrown out of use entirely, but it is better not to use them at all than to make any mistake in their use. There is a common practice of bespattering country houses with these fantastically cut shingles which is one of the most deplorable mistakes that is made in suburban architecture. It is more difficult to use fancy shingles properly than one would suppose.

SHEATHING: The building to be sheathed on the outside frame with good, sound fa" matched hemlock boards, not to exceed 10" in width, nailed with three tenpenny nails to every bearing. These boards to be placed on the frame horizontally.

All partitions throughout the building to be set according to the plans. Bearing partitions on first floor to foot upon the girders below, and be capped with plate for the bearing of the second story joists. Bearing partitions in the second story to foot upon the plate. The studs at angles to be thoroughly spiked together before being placed in position. All doors and windows 3' 0" wide and over, to be trussed over the top thoroughly and substantially. All partitions to be sized to a straight edge, joists in all cases to be doubled up under all partitions. Grounds put on for finish throughout the building where necessary. In setting door and window studs, arrange so that casings will fill in each case. If any second story or attic partitions do not set over partitions below they should be substantially trussed to prevent sagging.

The sheathing on the outside of the frame should be carefully put on in such a manner that there be no cracks nor holes. Special attention must be paid to the loose knots, which are liable to fall out after the sheathing boards are put in place. The narrower the sheathing boards the better, but the above is the common width used. After years of careful experiment it is now quite an accepted fact that the stiffest house is produced by putting on the sheathing boards horizontally, and not diagonally. There is a great deal more waste in the diagonal method, and the nailings are further apart. It is very important that the trussing over window and door heads should be attended to, otherwise the superincumbent weight may settle the heads in such a manner that the doors and sashes will not fit. Equally important it is that the partitions not supported below by other partitions should be trussed properly. Of course the partitions should come over each other, but this is sometimes impracticable.

The use of wire nails has become quite general and is commended by good mechanics.

LUMBER: The lumber used throughout the building to be white pine, unless otherwise specified. All of the exterior finishing lumber to be composed of first-class pine lumber; all inside finishing lumber to be clear and dry, free from sap, shakes, or knots.

Exterior Finish: All of the exterior finish for corner boards, windows, and door casings, cornices, water tables, piazza finish, bands, sidings, and all manner of other finish, shown on plans and details to be composed of lumber, as above specified, and primed as soon as put up. The exterior of the surface of the buildings, where required by the plans, to be covered with dressed first-class clapboards, 4" weather face of white pine, as specified under the head of lumber. Corner boards 3" X 4", i% "with molding returned around tops. Shadow or band courses over windows all around, as per detail. Exterior base 6", with water table cap. The ceiling and the piazza columns, which are also to be of yellow pine, are to be finished natural wood.

There is nothing better than white pine for the interior trim, where an inexpensive natural finish is desired, or for exterior woodwork where the same is painted. It is verycommon to use white wood or poplar for interior woodwork, treating with stain, so that it shall imitate some other darker and finer wood. This is dishonest, and on the very face of it is a sham; better not have any woodwork in the house excepting pine, than to be caught hoodwinking your friends with imitation work.

The most picturesque frame houses that are built are shingled all over, and the shingles stained colors to suit. There is every argument in favor of shingles rather than clapboards. Shingles lap over each other in such a manner as tobe three thicknesses in any part of the work, and are nailed very often, while clapboards lap but an inch or two, and the nailings are 16" apart (at every stud). It stands to reason that shingles give the best protection. Then, too, there is the charming effect of the deep, soft coloring, which can only be had with stained shingles.

PIAZZAS: Construct all porches or piazzas in strict accordance with the detail and working drawings prepared for the same. Form all cornices, railings, columns, capitals, etc., with exactness, and in conformity with the full size sections for same.

Cornices: All cornices to be constructed in accordance with the working drawings for same. Stock moldings may be used throughout. All gutters must be carefully graded to run all the water to the required outlets, and the same to be put up in a substantial manner.

Building PAPER: The entire exterior surface of the building to be covered with building paper, well put on the sheathing boards, joints well lapped and secured with laths nailed to each stud. Flash under frames. Use the Mica Roofing Co.'s No. 1 building paper.

The matter of gutters is a very important one, and should be looked after very carefully. There are many methods of forming gutters on and in the roof; these are lined with tin, and the owner is dependent entirely upon the stability of the tin to secure his roof against leaking and rotting away. Every year now, hanging gutters or eave troughs are becoming more and more popular. They hang clear of the roof, and can be easily replaced at any time; if they leak it can be easily detected, and there is with them no danger of a leak injuring the material of the roof or anything outside of the house.

Among the many building papers which are now flooding the markets, it is a difficult matter to choose any one that is really the best. The brands manufactured by the Mica Roofing Co., of New York, are probably the best to be had.

Porch columns made of yellow pine, and treated with spar varnish, in the natural color of the wood, are much sought after, and if the columns are sufficiently massive the effect is very good. There is nothing better than the good old Doric column for a simple one, or the Ionic if a more elaborate pattern is desired.

ROOFS: Cover all the roofs, including those of porch, *piazza.,* etc., with good hemlock shingling strips 1" X 3" in size, and *2)4"* apart, well nailed to every rafter. All the rough carpentry necessary to form the projection of the eaves, as required for all cornices, gutters, etc., to be done in accordance with the plans and details. All to be composed of good, sound lumber, and put on in a good substantial manner.

Slate: Use only first-class black slate of manufacture. These to be in size, properly laid and cut neatly around all hips and valleys. Use galvanized iron nails, and take great care to have the flashings properly put in so as to guarantee an absolutely first-class job.

Shingles: All roofs to be covered with the best quality of sawed cedar shingles, laid 5 ⅝" to the weather. All plain butts. Shingles in all gables and on all walls where shown.

Where the roofs are to be shingled, it is much better to cover the rafters with shingling strips, put on two or three inches apart. The space between the strips admits the air in such a manner that the shingles dry off much more quickly after they have been soaked with the rain, which could not possibly occur if the shingles were laid on close boards. If the water from the roof is to be collected and stored in a filtering cistern for domestic use, it is much better to have the roofs of slate, and in case they are used the specifications should call for boards on roof and felt lining, but, where good water can be had from other sources, the cedar shingles make an admirable roof, lasting for years, and one which, if left to the effects of the weather, will soon become a most charming silver gray. If cedar shingles are not available, white pine shingles may be substituted, but if pine shingles are left to the weather they turn a brownish black and do not look nice. If pine shingles are used they may be treated with one coat of raw linseed oil and plumbago. This oil and plumbago, by the way, is a most admirable preservative as well as a good slate color. The Cabot and Dexter stains are the best preservatives.

FLOORS: All floors, where not otherwise specified, to be of white pine free from sap, shakes, black, unsound, or loose knots, tongued and grooved 5" thick, not over 4" wide, all well and secret nailed to every joist.

The porch floors to be of white pine i£" thick, and face to be well laid in white lead. Attic to be floored all over and closely fitted to the timbers. The first story, bathroom, and second story hall floors to be of Southern pine, ⅞" thick and 3" face, and all other floors required by the plans to be composed of lumber the best of the kind specified; all to be tongued and grooved, and all secret nailed to each joist; all joints to be neatly smoothed up, and the finished surface left suitable for the painter to finish. The laundry, servant's water closet, and cold room to be floored. Neatly miter borders around all hearths.

If carpets are to be used throughout the first story, it will not be necessary to have the floors of Southern pine, but nowadays everyone is so fond of rugs that it is usual to provide for hard pine floors for the first story at least.

As a matter of fact, the Southern pine can be had at prices which equal white pine flooring, so that it is a matter of no additional expense to use that class of hard pine, if desired.

If an especially fine floor is desired, quarter sawn, or combgrained flooring of oak should be clearly mentioned, and the floors should all be lined with hemlock or other 7/fa" surfaced boards laid on the studs diagonally. This lining or rough flooring will answer for the masons to plaster from, and after the plastering is dry the finish flooring may be laid. A hard wood floor should be laid with an 18" border running all around the room and following all breaks and angles. All flooring should be perfectly dry, and should be laid with great care to insure perfect work. The workmen must be cautioned again and again about defacing the floors.

The ornamental metal work for exterior cornices, etc. (see cut p. 3) can be had of J. T. Wagner, 108 Chambers Street, New York.

DOORS: All doors in the house, except where otherwise specified, to be made of clear white pine, free from sap, and must be well made, and first-class. Size of doors to be marked on floor plans with width, height, etc. All doors may be 4 panel stock doors excepting those in the first story which will be cross-panel, and 5 panels each. All flush molded, both faces, and made with concealed tenons. FRONT DOORS: The front, vestibule, and outside doors to be made as detailed; to be of white pine 1" thick. Plate glass where shown, and the front and vestibule doors to have raised mold, both faces. Size of doors for widths and heights as per floor plans.

Inside DOORS: All inside doors to be first-class flush molded, made of best white pine, and to be 14" thick 4 panel stock doors, excepting principal rooms first story. Sliding door 1"; 8 panels. Cellar doors are to be first-class battened doors, put together with screws and of two thicknesses #j" X 5" flooring. All doors double faced.

Sash Doors—Jambs—Thresholds: All doors marked on the plans; sash doors to have proper rebates for receiving glass and suitable provisions for same with beads, etc. Use il/&" door jambs; hard wood molded thresholds and turned stops.

DWARF DOORS: All necessary dwarf doors to be provided where needed, for all pantries, closets, sinks, etc., these to be paneled. All dwarf doors to be composed of clear white pine and to be il/% " thick.

Cellar DOORS: Outside cellar door required by the plans, to be made of two thicknesses of fa" ceiling boards, hung to strong plank frames. Hatchway doors same.

As doors made to special designs cost nearly double what the stock doors cost, it is a matter of economy to do away with special doors as far as possible. It is very important that the doors shall be of first-class workmanship, and that the material from which they are made shall be thoroughly kiln-dried, otherwise it would be found that after a year's use the doors will be warped out of shape, or will have shrunk so much that the locks will not catch in the striking plates. If there are to be any hard wood doors they should be made "staved up. " By "staved up" is meant glued up of small square staves. The hard wood should be veneered on.

HARDWARE—BUTTS: Hang all doors throughout with loose joint butts, of sufficient size to throw them clear of architraves. All doors over 7' high to have 3 butts each. Butts on front and vestibule and outside doors to be 43" X 4" bronze.

Use ball tipped butts throughout. Butts on all inside doors to be 4" X 4" butts. All dwarf doors throughout to have suitable butts to match other furniture, and all door butts to have loose joints. The cellar doors to have strong wrought-iron hinges with hooks and staples, and all trapdoors, if any, to have the necessary flush rings to raise doors. Cellar hatchway to have fastening bar on inside. Hang sliding doors on door hangers.

KNOBS, ROSES, AND ESCUTCHEONS: The front and vestibule doors to have bronze ball knobs, roses, and escutcheons. All other outside doors to have ball knobs, roses, etc. All inside doors, except as noted, to have ball knobs, roses, etc. Put suitable knobs on all dwarf doors, press doors, etc. Use the Bardsley wood knobs throughout the second story and attic. The front and outside doors to have mortised bolts. All hardware and trimmings required and not specially cited to be furnished in conformity with the other work.

It is a very good idea for the owner to purchase direct from the dealers the finishing hardware for doors and windows, instead of leaving the matter to the contractor. By doing this the owner has the choice, and can select whatever he thinks desirable. Bronze hardware all through the house is best, if the expense is not in the way. For the second story and attic the wood knobs are much liked. In selecting the hardware for a house one can depend upon it that the plainer and more simple the design, the more lasting will be the satisfaction. The present hardware market is full of all manner of designs, a majority of which are far from being artistic.

The Bardsley wood knobs are well made and are to be relied on for good wear. The Stanley steel butts are also excellent, and may be had in several different finishes. The mortise bolts above specified are often omitted, being considered useless.

Locks: Front and vestibule doors to have 6" anti-friction front door locks with two keys, and to have brass front and striking plates. The keys to pass both front and vestibule doors. All other outside doors to have a good 34" mor-tise lock, with brass front and striking plates. Sliding doors to have bronze cups, locks, etc., complete to correspond with rebate or astragal. All small closets, presses, drawers, etc., to have suitable locks as approved. All door locks throughout to be mortise locks, and of manufacture. Hang pantry doors on double-acting spring hinges of manufacture.

BLIND HINGES: The outside blinds to be hung on approved outside blind hinges, and trimmed with the appropriate appliances for fastening, and adjusting.

WARDROBE HOOKS: Put two rows of wardrobe hooks in all closets; and all other hardware and trimmings to make the whole job of work complete to be furnished of the best kind specified. The wardrobe hooks to be double.

The hardware for a Colonial house has received the special attention of the most skillful designers in the business, and consequently it is an easy matter for anyone to procure exactly the right thing for each purpose.

For sliding doors there are the Warner (overhead) hangers, made by E. C. Stearns, Syracuse, N. Y. The Lane door hangers (Po'keepsie, N. Y.), and the Barry hangers, all of which act very easily, are not difficult to adjust, and give good satisfaction; 3" must be allowed for them to work in. The double-acting, self-closing hinges made by J. Bardsley, New York, are to be depended upon, and in wood knobs, roses, and escutcheons there is to be found nothing better than the knobs made by the same house. The Russel & Erwin Manufacturing Co., of New York, and the Allentown Hardware Co., Pennsylvania, are manufacturers of some of the best made and most artistic lines of hardware. Blind hinges should be of wrought iron, and angle hinges, and the Domestic Blind Adjuster is a good appliance for holding the blind either open or shut or at any angle.

Window Frames: All window frames constructed to correspond with the working drawings as usual for the same. To be made box frames, and fitted for weights; frames all made of clear white pine well seasoned. The cellar windows to be constructed of 2" plank in accordance with the detail drawings for same. For size of glass see elevations. All sash shown "single" to be hung on the top with butts for same, and each to have proper bolt and adjuster. Windows to have 4" X 1", exterior casings. Pulley stiles *fa"* counter sills, etc. House the jambs, etc. Carpenter to have the frames properly primed before same leave the shop.

Sash: The sash to be 1" thick, and hung on "Sampson Spot" sash cord, weights, and noiseless axle pulleys. Sash for plate glass to be 2" thick. These sash to have weatherlipped Meeting rail, acorn mold sash bars. Sash in cellar windows to be 1" thick and to be hung on back flaps and secured with hooks and staples. All sash to have burglarproof sash locks, and lifts of bronze in the principal rooms both first and second stories. Elsewhere japanned. Each lower sash to have flush sash lift of plain bronze. Sash 2' 6" wide and over to have two lifts—smaller sash to have one lift.

See to it that the weights for sash are properly adjusted to balance exactly. Nothing is more provoking than an unevenly balanced sash.

If special guard is considered necessary, the cellar window frames may be fitted with *y2"* iron, 3" or 4" apart, let into frames.

The "Sampson" sash cord mentioned above has received the test of a number of years' use, and proved itself to be among the best of the many found in the market. It is made by The Sampson Cordage Co. The Pullman Sash Balance is getting quite popular. It does away with box frames and in many ways is admirable.

The Ives Patent Sash Lock (New Haven, Conn.) is one of the best in the market, and will defy all efforts at opening from the outside. Sash lifts are more important than might appear at first. Many a lower sash has been ruined by continued lifting at the meeting rail.

GLASS: The window sash to be glazed with first-class selected double thick glass, to be well bedded, bradded, back puttied, and cleaned off. The cellar windows to have same glass. Stained glass to be furnished by owner. BLINDS: All windows to have outside rolling blinds, made of best white pine. Hang with wrought iron angle butts, and furnish each blind with fastener and Domestic blind adjuster.

If it is desired to have plate glass in a door or two, or the principal windows of the house, it should be clearly mentioned in the specifications above, or marked on the elevations thus, "plate"; and stained glass, if there is to be any, should also be likewise mentioned, although it is better for the owner to purchase stained glass and have contractor set the same.

In order that the house may be kept cool in the summer time, there should be outside rolling blinds on all of the windows; inside blinds will not 'do the work for country houses. The radiation of the sun against the glass is the source of the main bulk of the heat in the summer time; the inside blinds do not prevent this, while the outside blinds do. The only substitute that can be used for blinds are awnings, which are the most desirable appliances for keeping out the heat and the glare of the sun. If it is decided to use awnings on any of the windows, the outside blinds may as well be omitted, thus saving some little expense. Awnings are in summer really the best protection against the violence of the sun's heat, because of the good circulation which is possible through the openings at the bottom, and, too, they add considerable to the exterior effect.

The above blind adjuster is a capital appliance for adjusting blinds to any angle that may be required.

Interior Finish: All to be constructed as required by the plans and details, with sound, clear, kiln-dried white pine, unless otherwise specified. All put up with neat close joints, smoothed up and well sand-papered. Base put down in all apartments not wainscoted. Beads to be put on all corners. Base 8" molded throughout, except closets, where 6" O. G. Door and window trim pilaster finish. Base and turned corner blocks; all stock 5%" rebated stool with apron,

made of casing returned at each end. There will be a fa" wall mold around all casings, same to member into base mold. Sweeping strips 3/£" quarter round, put down around base and door in all apartments.

Pilaster finish is better explained by the accompanying cut than any other way. The advantage of the corner block arises from the fact that there is but little chance for the head and side casings to shrink away from each other. The base block being thicker than the casing, receives the base and base mold very nicely, and, being a plain beveled block, is not so liable to be injured by the marks of passing feet.

The molding used for pilaster casing can be had in almost any planing mill 'and, in houses of moderate cost, it is perhaps the neatest trim to be selected. The "sweeping strip" is a great saving for the housekeeper, and the "wall mold" fills out neatly any inequalities of the plaster.

Stairs: All stairways to be built where located on plans. The main staircase to be built and supported on strong plank strings, the risers to be 1", and the treads 1%" thick. Dimensions in all cases for height of risers and widths of treads to be measured from the building. All stairs must be put up after the plastering is dry. Main staircase to have Georgia pine treads, landings, and risers.

Newels, Rails, And Balusters: The newels, rails, and balusters, and other details involved in same, for main staircase to be of selected dry, quarter sawn oak worked in accordance with the detail drawings. All outside steps to be built on good, strong plank strings, provided with 1" plank steps and 1" risers of white pine well put up and thoroughly secured.

Mantels: To be furnished by owner and set by contractor.

There will be a 2" picture rail as per detail fitted and put in all of the rooms of the house excepting in attic, kitchen, closets, pantries, and laundry. This is to be of pine, or of wood to correspond with finish.

As all of the hard woods are about the same price, any one that is preferred

may be selected for the newels, rails, and balusters of the stairs, but there is nothing better for a hall than oak. Of course, it would be much nicer to have the entire stairway, including the strings, treads, and riders, built of hard wood but for the expense connected therewith.

Special attention must be given to the condition of dryness of the plastering before the stairs, which are really cabinet work, are brought in the building. A little dampness will ruin ever so good a piece of work. As written above, the rear, attic, and cellar stairs would be built of white pine.

If you want mantels of good design and of first-class construction go to J. S. Conover & Co., or Robt. C. Lowry, New York, where you can also find everything necessary for the fireplace, including tile, grates, fenders, andirons, etc. Some Western firms are very reliable and furnish first class goods. The Aldine Mfg. Co., of Grand Rapids, is one of them.

A picture rail is a great saving in the wear of walls.

Closets: The closets are to be fitted up with beaded cleats for the reception of wardrobe hooks. Shelves over hooks as desired, and as marked on plans. There will be drawers in closets.

Butler's Pantry—Cupboards— Kitchen Dressers, Etc.: The butler's pantry to be fitted up with white pine shelves, to be placed on all available sides, 4 shelves on each side; above counter shelf to be of " lumber with turned standards from bottom to top for support when necessary. Build a counter shelf 2' 10" high, and 20" wide by 1j" thick as shown, under which arrange for lockers inclosed with panel doors and drawers. Also furnish all trimmings for the full and proper completion of the pantry as per drawings. The cupboards to be inclosed with sliding sash doors. Build drip, etc., complete for butler's sink.

The kitchen pantry to be fitted with white pine shelves to be placed on all available sides; 4 shelves on each side, to be of #$" lumber with turned supports where necessary. The lower shelf to be 20" wide and high enough above floor to receive a flour barrel.

Construct kitchen dresser in same manner as specified for butler's cupboards.

The cut shown herewith explains the method of treatingthe dresser in the kitchen. If drawers are required, they may substitute the lockers. A very excellent contrivance for a pantry is the tipping bin. (The arrangement of the butler's pantry is shown on p. 12.)

Kitchen SINK: The sink to be ceiled up underneath with narrow beaded battens, and provided with door of same. Ceil up for a splash back 16" high over sink, with narrow beaded batten, and cap same as wainscoting. Build drip board as shown.

Wainscoting: Wainscot walls of kitchen with beaded ceiling 3" wide, and cap with a neat beveled and molded cap. All wainscoting to be 3' 6" high. Same in bath room and water closet.

COLD AIR DUCT: Construct a frame of 2" plank, to be built in the underpinning where marked on plans, to admit cold air to furnace, cover with coarse wire netting; construct a cold air box from this opening to furnace with pine flooring /&' X 5"; make air-tight, and to suit requirements. Put in a slide damper inside of cellar wall, and make the whole job complete.

Wood Partitions In Cellar: To be built with 2" X 4" studs, 16" from centers; board up to ceiling with flooring fy" X 5" of good white pine. Sills and plates to be 4" X 4", and put all up after concrete floor is laid. Cold room in cellar to be fitted up with 4 shelves all around.

It is a much better method to use a kitchen sink with iron legs, and not inclose it at all. A locker under the kitchen sink is a resort for odds and ends, for oil cans, discarded utensils, and clouts, and a place never fit to be looked into.

The wainscot in the kitchen is almost indispensable, and if the plastering is carried down to the floor behind the wainscot, there is no reason why insects of any kind should make the wainscot their headquarters. If desired, the butler's pantry could also be wainscoted with good results, and if wanted, should

be added to the specifications as well as the wainscot of hall or any other room.

The cold room in cellar is generally laid out to go near the foot of the cellar stairs, and is usually but a large closet, with a window for ventilation, in which butter and stores are kept.

TINNING: All angles, valleys, gutters, decks, etc., in all roofs to be covered with the best Meurer Roofing tin. The gutters to be properly lined; run the tin up under the shingles at least 8"; bring the tin over the face and tack it down smoothly. All tinning throughout to be well soldered in resin and made perfectly water-tight.

Conductors of galvanized iron to be put up as indicated on plans with all necessary curves, breaks, bends, etc., to carry the water from the several roofs to the ground.

The conductors to be of 3" caliber, and thoroughly secured with iron hooks. Where the tin comes against the chimneys the tin must turn up into the bricks and be thoroughly secured with gas hooks. All proper and necessary places to be flashed whether specified or not, and everything requisite to make all places water-tight must be done; all leaks to be stopped after other craftsmen, and everything left perfectly water-tight at the completion of the building.

Run from rear gutters as shown, through roof, properly flashing at these points; connect with 3" pipe, and run into tank. Line tank with 12 oz. tinned copper. Make all perfectly tight, and furnish with overflow connections through the roof to the nearest conductor leading to the ground.

If hanging gutters or "eaves troughs" are thought desirable it should be mentioned in the specifications. Plecker's Corrugated Conductor and Long Eaves Trough (made of either copper or galvanized iron) manufactured by Clark, Quien & Morse, of Peoria, 111., are well made and very serviceable.

The rear gutters are often located sufficiently far upon the roofs so that the water collected by them may be conducted to the tank in the attic.

The tin plates made by the Meurer

Bros. Co., Brooklyn, N. Y., can be depended upon to give good satisfaction, especially the brand above mentioned. Should there be any tin roofs use the "Meurer Roofing."

Painter's Specifications. PAINTING: All the materials used throughout the building to be furnished and of the best quality, and all labor to be performed for the full and complete painting of the building.

All the exterior woodwork must have two good coats of Asbestos paint, colors as chosen and directed by owner. Paint all the tin and galvanized iron work with two coats Prince's Metallic Paint. Putty up all the woodwork smoothly after priming. Shingles on roofs to be treated with one coat of plumbago and raw oil. (The painting includes all exterior shingles, except on roofs.) The priming must be done as fast as exterior woodwork is put up. The ceiling of piazzas and porches, the front and vestibule doors, and the *piazza,* columns to be finished natural wood with a coat of filler and two coats of All the inside work must be painted with two good coats as above mentioned, in such colors or tints as directed, excepting as otherwise specified.

Probably no better house paint can be found than "Asbestos Paint," manufactured by H. W. Johns & Co., New York, and for metal work there is nothing better than "Prince's Metallic."

Where shingles are used in the walls and gables of houses there is no more charming method of handling them, than to stain them with a good shingle stain. The Creosote Stain, made by Samuel Cabot, Boston, and the English stains of Dexter Brothers, Boston, are highly recommended, and besides producing lovely colors, are the best preservatives known. If, before putting on the shingles, they are dipped in these stains, the most lasting and satisfactory effects are secured. Examine any old roof and you will find that the shingles have rotted away more in the inside than on the exposed surfaces. Now by dipping the shingles in a good preservative the inside or concealed portion is just as well protected as the outside surface.

This also applies to roofs, and no such coloring can be produced by paint as that of these stains, which are deep, warm, and rich, or of the most subtle grays. Plumbago and raw oil make a capital roof paint if an ordinary gray color is desired.

All of the pine finish and doors, first and second stories, to have one coat pure spirit shellac white, rubbed down with oo sand paper, and to have two coats

Wood Finish Interior, neatly rubbed down with a pumice stone and water to a smooth and dead finish. All of the main stairs, main hall, parlor, and dining room to have floors finished with Floor Var nish. The hard wood to be treated same as pine excepting it is to have a coat of Wheeler's Filler and an extra coat of varnish.

The "rough cast" walls are to have a coat of size and to be painted with zinc paint colors to suit owner. At completion the painted walls should be perfectly dead and flat, and show no glossy, oily, or greasy surfaces.

'Rough cast" walls painted in oil with flat tints make the most lasting, sensible, and sanitary walls that could be put in a house. The owner has any color at his disposal, and each room may be different from the others, and yet harmonious with all; several colors may be used in a room, for there are two distinct parts to the walls, the ground below the picture rail, and the frieze above, these with the ceiling give chances for three colors or tones. The better way to arrange the colors is to use three shades of a color in a room, grading the shades from darker to lighter, for instance, the ground might be the darker, the frieze a shade lighter, and the ceiling lightest of all.

Wheeler's Filler, made by the Bridgeport W. F. Co., the Murphy & Co.'s Varnishes and those made by Berry Bros, are thoroughly reliable materials, and may be depended upon to present a fine appearance for years.

A very artistic decoration may be used on the frieze by sending to Fr. Beck & Co., New York, for their relief ornaments in the shape of festoons, gar-

lands, and wreaths. These may be easily applied to the plaster walls, and when decorated in light colors are very charming and graceful (See frieze in sketch of dining room china closet, p. 29).

GAS FITTER'S SPECIFICATIONS. GAS FITTING: Use best wrought-iron gas pipe of the various sizes required. The mains to be run as direct as possible, and so graded that any water gathering in pipes can be run out at a convenient point in the cellar. No pipe to be less than *ffi'* for any fixture connection, and larger for any chandelier having four burners or over. Secure all piping substantially in place with iron hold-fasts, and secure the drop and other outlets with galvanized iron straps and screws; the pipes to be run to supply burners where indicated. The side wall bracket connections to be arranged so as to project from finished wall at right angles, and the proper distance for same; and pipe ends for drop lights to hang and set perfectly straight and plumb.

All joints to be put together in red lead; all pipes to be capped, proven tight, and cap left on. Provide all necessary shut-offs, and make a perfect job. Timbers not to be cut except where strictly necessary, and no timber to be cut through center of span. Carpenter to do all cutting and fitting.

The above paragraph is generally not used in suburban houses because there is usually no gas supply, and private gas machines are generally deemed too expensive. There are, however, many arguments to be brought forward in favor of private gas machines, for instance the saving in labor in taking care of and the wear and tear on the number of lamps required to light the house; diminution of danger; convenience, and the superior lighting, which is secured by the gas.

As a matter of fact a gas machine is a good investment, if one has the money for it. Close estimates of the value of the daily labor necessary to keep up a bevy of lamps; the cost of breakage, etc., and the cost of oil would be found to exceed the expense of gasoline and running the gas machine, plus a fair rate of interest on the three or four hundred dollars ex-

pended for the same.

Happy is the man who is fortunate to have a home in a town where there is a good service of electric light! Incandescent electric light is the acme of all methods of lighting; requiring no care; always ready; never impairing the air in the room; no heat; no odors; perfections of neatness, and steady as clocks.

Whether gas or electric light is used fixtures will have to be had, and fortunately these fixtures are now so inexpensively made that almost anyone can afford to have them. A well designed and graceful chandelier or electrolier is one of the most charming furnishings of the house. It may be so because it is pendent and in that portion of the room which could not be otherwise furnished. The Oxley & Enos Manufacturing Co. , 275 Fifth Avenue, New York, and the Mitchell, Vance Co., 836 Broadway, New York, are the people who make the most picturesque fixtures.

If electric light is to be used great precaution must be taken with the wiring in order that all chance of danger be avoided. Thorough insulation must be effected, and the best method by which to accomplish this is by means of conduits made of non-conducting material, through which all wires should be run. The Board of Underwriters should pass upon all electric wiring work, where a regular superintendent is not employed.

Plumber's Specifications.

Plumbing specifications for a frame dwelling to be built for according to the plans and specifications hereto attached.

All material, fixtures, and workmanship to be first-class in every respect, and, in case not satisfactory to the owner, to be removed and replaced at the contractor's expense. The entire work must be completed in every particular, and must be perfect in its sanitary conditions and arrangements. The plumber does not have to put down well, cistern, or cesspool, nor has he anything to do with the drain pipe outside of the house; all work outside of the walls of the house will be done by other contractors, unless otherwise specified.

These specifications are intended to cover the plumbing in the house where there is no public or city water supply, and where a tank in the attic is required for the storage of the water pumped in the tank from either or both cistern or well; should there be a city water supply, the following clause should be inserted in place of that referring to the connection of the well, cistern, and tank.

The plumber to give the proper authorities the requisite notices relating to his work; obtain official permits for tapping the main in the street, and license for temporary obstructions, and pay all proper fees for the same; these to include charges for tapping. The house to be feet back from curb. Water to be brought from the street to the house; "galvanized iron pipe with lever handle stop and waste cock on inside of cellar wall; galvanized iron pipe to be used only to get the water from main to house. Contractor to dig trench for water pipe only, and fill in the same. Put a cock on the main in a place convenient for a lawn sprinkler.

It is better plumbing to bring the water from the street to the house through strong lead pipe—the galvanized iron pipe being used only to save expense. If a lawn sprinkler and hose is desired, the specifications should be made to call for same in addition to the above.

General Notes—Stripping: All service pipes to he put on 1" stripping, in all cases prepared by the contractor, who is also to do all cutting, etc. All pipes in house to be put up so as to be easily accessible for examination.

Fastenings—Connections—Protection: Secure all lead pipes with hard metal tacks and screws, and make all connections between iron and lead pipes through brass ferrules, which must be soldered to the lead pipes, calked with oakum, and run molten lead into the iron hubs. Properly encase in asbestos covering, and pack around with mineral wool, in boxes and cases, all water pipes, traps, where the same are in exposed places. The joints in all iron pipe to be calked with oakum, run with molten lead, and thoroughly calked. All joints in lead pipe to be carefully and neatly wiped joints, and not soiled or painted.

Main SUPPLY: Tap the tank in attic, and run down through bath room and butler's pantry with a 2" strong lead pipe, leaving out branches for the separate work. Put in shut-off cocks in handy places, also cocks in cellar for draining all the works in the house. And all pipes to be properly graded so as to drain off. (The 2" supply pipe herein mentioned, to be attached to pump and from pump to well so that one pipe will carry the water both to and from the tank. If there is also a cistern, attach same to pump with a 2" pipe and put in under the sink a three-way cock with a lever handle so that water may be pumped from either sink or well.

In getting a first-class plumbing job the integrity and personal character of the plumber will have to be depended upon, if the owner is his own superintendent. Architects with an experience of a score of years will tell you that sanitary plumbing work is the most difficult of all their superintendence. There are so many methods of setting up and connecting each fixture that the expert is often bothered to decide which is the best.

The mineral wool above specified can be had of the U. S. Mineral Wool Co. of New York, and is capital material for filling in any partition wall for the purpose of keeping out the cold.

SOIL PIPES: Connect with drain pipe to cesspool or sewer a 4" cast-iron pipe; continue up through bath room where shown to a point 2' o" above roof, where cap with ventilating hood. Leave out branches of proper sizes for all the different works. Make all connections with Y branches and bends. Secure and support properly all cast-iron pipes with hooks, braces, or hangers. WATER-CLOSETS: The Sanitas closets are to be used. Contractor to fit up properly, connect with soil pipes with 6 pound lead bends. Supply cisterns through $/&" strong lead with cocks to control supply. The servant's water-closet to be a plain wash-out closet.

Cisterns to be cased in paneled oak or other hard wood, and the closets to have seat, cover, and back complete in same wood as cistern.

TEST: Before any plastering is done, contractor is to plug up all openings of wastes or vent pipes; fill the same with water from the highest point, and leave full one day, so that owner may see that all are tight. Should any leak occur, it must be made tight. All cast-iron pipes to have a good coating of coal tar inside and out before being placed in position. There are so many hundreds of patterns and kinds of water closets that it is not easy to choose any paticular ones. The Smith & Anthony Co. is a first-rate concern, and the owner will find himself safe in their hands. The "Sanitas" closets are thoroughly reliable and commendable, and are all open and free from casings. It is by far the best method to have all the plumbing and fixtures open and without casing. If anything should happen to any part it is better to know it at once, rather than to have it concealed until the health of the family has been damaged.

The paragraph in regard to testing the pipes will relieve the owner's mind considerably, and it can be applied so simply that anyone may use it.

Care must be exercised with all horizontal runs of lead pipe and the same must be supported on little ledges or shelves their entire length.

Boiler And Range Connections: Plumber to make all connections between boiler and water back of range, setting each in place and making all complete. Range to be furnished by owner.

Pumps: Fit up complete in kitchen a 2" double chambered pump of Colman manufacture. Build a lead safe under same, and drain safe into waste in cellar. Put in a three-way cock to draw water from either well or cistern. In the rising main to the tank place check valve just above sink supply, so that fresh water may be pumped directly into the sink, and so that servants cannot draw cold water from tank.

Tank, Pipes, Etc.: (Note; tinner to line same.) Put in a $j4"$ tell-tale from the tank near top to kitchen sink near force pump. Put in a " air pipe connected with supply main under the tank, then carry up to the top of the tank and form a hook end, discharging into the water.

By turning the handle of the three-way cock, water can be had from either well or cistern through the one pump. The check valve placed as above mentioned will automatically oblige the servant to do her own pumping for cold water and, at the same time, one can get fresh water directly from the well instead of having to draw it from the tank.

The Colman pump is a very well-made machine, taking up but little room, and may be manipulated by a child. The tell-tale will announce the fact that the tank is full but not how nearly full. An ingenious contrivance may be put up by any plumber which will indicate the height of water in the tank. A bit of chain attached to a float in the tank is carried down through the partition to the kitchen where a small ball holds it taut, as the water rises or falls the ball indicates on a cardboard fastened behind it. The wood work of the tank is built by the carpenter, and it should be located and arranged so as to have good support by the partitions below.

BOILER: The boiler to be a 40 gallon galvanized iron of Ronalds & Co.'s manufacture, dome head, set on single legged stool. Contractor to set boiler and supply with water through $y\pm''$ strong lead pipe, and connect to water back of range with strong lead pipe and brass couplings. To have " sediment cock and pipe. This pipe connected with nearest waste, so as to empty and cleanse boiler; also place a $fy\&''$ stop cock on supply pipe and relief pipe from top of boiler to tank. CIRCULATION: There must be a $\%''$ strong lead pipe connected to hot-water pipe at highest point, and to run down below boiler and there connect to sediment pipe inside sediment cock for the purpose of circulation of hot water. There must be no depression in any pipes, and hot water must be kept rising from head of boiler.

Copper boilers are preferred by many people, but are omitted here because of expense both of cost and of labor in keeping them in order. The galvanized boiler is fully as strong, and, if neatly finished by the painter to correspond with adjoining woodwork, presents a very neat and orderly appearance. The boiler may be connected with range with copper or nickel-plated pipes, with small additional cost. The device for circulating the water is for the purpose of insuring a copious supply of hot water. Perhaps nothing is more exasperating than to have to wait for your bath while the water is heating. The larger boiler one has the hotter and more abundant will be the hot water. It is common to find thirty gallon boilers in small houses, but they are taxed to their utmost capacity to do the work, and then often fail. Tinned brass pipes are used for hot water in more expensive houses.

It is often the case, in small houses, that the ordinary boiler is in the way or takes up too much room. To meet this the boiler is often hung with irons in a horizontal position over the range and high above it.

Sinks—Kitchen: The kitchen sink to be of galvanized iron 18" X 36". To have supplies through " strong lead pipes, and IJ4" wastes. To have hot and cold water for sink through flange and thimble bibbs of brass. One bibb to have screw for filler. Wastes to be 2", and to have Du Bois traps. The sink to have back and air chamber, and round iron legs.

Butler's Sink: Butler's sink of tinned copper 16" X 20", with marble slab with drip and back. Supply with hot and cold water through " strong lead pipe. Put in upright, nickel-plated pantry cocks, also nickel-plated chain, stay and plug. Sink to have 1-2" lead waste, and $y2''$ Du Bois trap.

The Du Bois traps herein referred to are plain lead traps fitted with a brass screw for cleaning out. Should it be decided to have the carpenter to inclose the kitchen sink the iron legs might be omitted.

The Sanitas Kitchen Sink and Flush-Pot was devised to overcome the difficult problem of the disposal of the kitchen waste. The fat and grease dissolved in water, generally hot, from the washing of dishes and utensils, quickly congeal and clog the waste pipes. Grease traps are commonly used to collect this grease, but these are difficult and disagreeable to manage. The Sanitas device is automatic in its action, and cannot do its work otherwise than completely and thoroughly.

To save expense the butler's sink may be mounted with a wood slab and drip; in some respects the wood is better, because it is not so easy to break glass and crockery on it as it is on the marble. Of course the marble may be protected with a rubber mat, etc., but these soon get foul.

The Kitchen Sinks known as the Blakeslee and the Demarest, with Back and Air Chamber, are the best.

Wash TRAYS: There will be a three part earthenware wash tray in laundry. These each to have supplies of hot and cold water through ffi' strong lead pipe with " tray bibbs (faucets). Fix each with $i4''$ brass plug and chain, and to have 2" wastes.with 2" Du Bois traps and connect with main 'soil line through 2" cast iron pipes. Trays to have ash frames and lids and iron standards.

Wash Basin: Where shown on plans. This will be 14" in diameter, of marble wedgwood ware set in counter sunk marble slab, and molded backs, with overflow complete. To have $y2''$ nickel-plated basin cocks, plug, chain stay, and chain all complete. Supply with hot and cold water through ffi' strong lead pipes, $1\%''$ wastes, $l\%''$ Sanitas trap, all properly connected with soil pipe. Support the slab with nickel-plated bracket or legs.

Do not put the wash trays in the kitchen, and have the earthenware trays by all means. The old-fashioned trays made of wood soon get foul and rank.

The oval basins 14" X 17" are better than the round ones, there is more elbow room, and the basin should not be cased in. Bibbs are perhaps more commonly called faucets. Stays are small rings to which the chain is fastened.

In order that the waste pipe from the trays—as well as the soil pipe from the cellar water closet—shall have the proper fall and yet go out through the wallabove the cellar bottom, it is a good plan to place both of these fixtures on a platform of wood about 7" above the top of the cellar concrete. This woodwork should be arranged for with the carpenter, and neither the platform nor fixtures should be located in the cellar until the concrete has had a chance to harden.

The Alberene Laundry Tubs are to be commended as first class sanitary fixtures. ’.

It is very common to have a slop-sink set up and connected in the attic or second story hall. These should have cold water supply.

Bath TUB; Where shown. To be 2’ o" X 6’ o" of 12-ounce tinned copper. Supply with hot and cold water through *fyfr"* strong lead pipe, and to have double hot and cold combination nickel-plated bath bibbs. Empty through 2" lead wastes and 2" Du Bois traps to main soil line. Have nickel-plated plug, chain, and chain stay. Overflow connections to branch into dips of traps throughout.

Ventilation: There must be lines of % " light lead pipes (back air pipes) run from the crowns of all traps and continued up to a point not less than 2’ o" above any waste connections, and there connected with main soil line by branches let out for that purpose. Where it is necessary to run the ventilating pipes a distance exceeding 5’ o" the traps must be vented with the McClellan Anti-Siphon Vent. These vents to be located in some convenient place near the fixtures, and connected with the crown of the trap with *y2"* light lead pipe, or if the plain traps and McClellan vents be *not* used, the Sanitas traps without vents will do the work.

The bath tub above mentioned is the old-fashioned affair, or at least it would be considered as such in the majority of modern houses of any pretension whatever. The popular tub is porcelain lined, and now that they are made at such reasonable prices they are likely to supplant the copper tubs entirely. One has only to pick up any one of the monthly magazines, and the advertising description and cuts of these luxurious baths will confront him. There are all kinds of patterns and shapes, and the most fastid-

ious can surely find something to suit. The majority of these new tubs have a bottom filling and waste arrangement, which does away with the old style of overhanging faucets, and the plug and chain, which things were always a nuisance. As is seen by the paragraph on "Ventilation," the object is to guard the water seal in the traps by one method or another. The best methods are "back airing," the use of the McClellan vent, or the use of the Sanitas trap, which it is claimed cannot be siphoned.

FLASHING: Wherever any vent or other pipes go through roof flash with sheet lead thoroughly, same fastened tightly to pipes so that no leak can occur. TRAPS: The wastes of all works to be trapped with separate Sanitas or Du Bois traps, as may be decided. Plumber to see that carpenter makes pockets in floor, etc., in order to get at said traps. Bibbs: All bibbs must be connected in a manner satisfactory to superintendent; also shut-off and waste cocks.

JOINTS: All soldered joints must be wiped joints, and this work done without soiling or painting. CHAINS: Chains for wash trays must be No. 2; for baths No. 1; for basins No. o. All to be nickel plated.

Lead PIPES: All lead pipe used in and throughout the building must weigh per lineal foot as follows:

Strong—",2 pounds; £4", 3 pounds; ",4 pounds; l", 5 pounds.

Light—1", 2 pounds; 1"’ 3 pounds; *1%", 3)4* pounds; *2",* 5 pounds; 3", 5 pounds.

The weights of lead pipe herein specified are suitable for an ordinary job, where the tank is depended upon for the supply, but should city water with its attendant high pressure be used, the weights of the lead pipe might have to be increased. The strong lead pipe above alluded to is for the hot and cold water supplies. The light is for wastes, vents, etc.

NOTE.—The gas fitting is generally done by the plumber, and perhaps should be inserted in the specifications made for the plumber. It is also common in country towns for the plumber to do the heating and range work, and

should such be the case the paragraphs on heating and range should also be incorporated.

It is also necessary that the gas piping should be extra large size throughout if it is intended to use the gasolene gas machines, which make a heavier and denser gas than that commonly supplied by the city companies.

SPECIFICATIONS of the heating, of the labor, and materials required for constructing the work for a frame dwelling, to be built for according to the plans hereto attached, and under the superintendence of the owner.

The specifications are intended to embrace the heating apparatus and kitchen range, together with all smoke pipes, tin hot air pipes, register boxes, registers, metal, lath, and dampers complete. Also all cartage, transportation, and labor of any kind, excepting only the mason and carpenter work involved. A No. with a "firepot of manufacture; same to have a galvanized iron case, and galvanized iron connections for cold air duct will be required. Contractor to furnish and set. The furnace must have a revolving and clinker-clearing grate.

SIZE OF PIPE AND REGISTERS: The hall, dining room, parlor, and library of the first story to have 10" pipes, and 12" X 15" registers. The butler’s pantry to have an 8" pipe, and 8" X 10" register. Principal rooms of the second story to have 9" pipes in cellar, excepting bath room, which is to have an 8" pipe. Second story rooms to have 10" X 14" registers; bath-room 8" X 10". The attic rooms to have 10" X 14" registers, and pipes for same in cellar to be 8",

Each room is to have an independent air pipe, and all hot air pipes are to be made double where they pass through floors or partitions or behind furrings. No square turns will be allowed, and all tin work to be of XX bright tin. All woodwork within 3" of any heater pipe, or within 16" of smoke pipe or the furnace, to be protected with sheets of bright tin. All registers to be of Tuttle & Bailey manufacture, or their equal; and in each case to be of black japanned. The furnace, the runs of the hot air pipes, and the registers are to be located as nearly as possible in the positions where shown on the plans.

COLD AIR DUCT: Cold air duct to be furnished and built by the carpenter, excepting the connection with furnace as before mentioned.

Finally: Furnish a check draft for the smoke pipe, besides an ordinary damper; also furnish a full set of fire tools, and a regulator of manufacture.

The old houses of Richardson & Boynton and-the Thatchei Furnace Co. , New York, are the best concerns in the country for the manufacture of furnaces. If the owner wishes to have an article *par excellence,* he will do well to put himself in direct communication with these houses. Should the owner decide to furnish the furnace himself he should change the specifications above to read accordingly.

One of the modern contrivances for house heating which is giving good satisfaction is the J. F. Pease "Economy" steam and warm air (combined) heaters. It has an advantage over direct steam in moderate weather when a slight fire will take "the chill off" the house without any great or violent heat.

Range: A No. range of manufacture with appliances will be required. Contractor to furnish and set complete. The connections between range and boiler to be made by plumber. The range to be portable, and to be fitted with a hood of wrought iron projection at least 6" beyond the size of the top of the range. Under this hood connect the vent flue with an 8" X 10" register. Put up smoke pipe of iron with damper complete. Protect all wood within 12" of range with zinc, and put down at least 12" of zinc on floor, to take place of hearth, both in front of range and on the sides.

Laundry Stove: A laundry stove No. of manufacture, with smoke pipe, protection, etc., complete, to be furnished and set in the (cellar) laundry.

Should it be decided to have a hearth of tile or slate the zinc might be omitted.

The regular laundry stove, with its arrangements for boiling clothes, its places for heating irons, etc., is a very convenient little fixture, and saves the kitchen from a lot of steam and heat.

SPECIFICATIONS of labor and materials required for constructing the electric bell work for a frame dwelling to be built for according to the plans hereto attached, and under the superintendence of the owner.

The bells for this house will be as follows:

Front door to the kitchen bell; also to second story bell, and the second story bell to be in hall with switch in convenient place.

Dining room to kitchen annunciator.

Library to kitchen annunciator.

Principal bedroom to kitchen annunciator.

The annunciator will be of first-class manufacture, with four drops labeled as follows: "Dining room," "Library," "Our room," "Side door."

The push button on the front door to be of plain bronze; same to correspond with front door hardware; side door to be same. The other wall buttons to be pearl and nickel plate, excepting in the dining room, where put down regular floor push button under table where directed, and furnish an attachment of flexible wire and pear push on the table so that the bell can be operated however far the table may be extended. There will also be an extra button in the principal bedroom same as before mentioned, said button operating a loud bell in the servant's room in attic.

Locate the batteries (Phoenix Dry Batteries) in the cellar in some convenient place where the owner can easily get at same. The batteries, wires, and all materials to be of the best quality, and the work to be done in a first-class manner.

Wherever necessary to remove the lath for putting in the wiring, the lath must be removed and replaced by the bell contractor.

In order to simplify matters, all the bells excepting that from front door to kitchen may be omitted, but a bell job such as the above calls for can be put in for a cost of thirtyfive dollars, and, considering the convenience, saving of steps, etc., that accompanies the use of the bells, it would be but poor policy to cut them away. The object in having the

front door button ring two bells, is to meet the objection of the servant being out, in which case the bell in second story hall can be heard.

CONTRACTS. CONTRACTS: The subject of contracts is one that cannot be treated in a very satisfactory manner, owing to the diversity in the law of the various States, and especially the great difference in the management of mechanics' liens. If the contractor is an honest and trustworthy party owning property in his own name you may depend upon it that there will be no trouble about liens, and with such a party you may get along very nicely with a short and brief contract or agreement, such as this:

Contract For Building: Made this day of, one thousand eight hundred and ninety-, by and between of the first part (the owner) and of the second part (the contractor) in these words: The part of the second part cove nant and agree to and with the said part of the first part,, to erect, construct, and finish in a good, substantial, and workmanlike manner the agreeable to the drawings and specifications hereto annexed, and to complete the said work by the day of, one thousand eight hundred and ninety-. And the part of the first part covenant and agree to pay unto the said part of the second part for the same the sum of dollars, for the true and faithful performance of all and every of the covenants and agreements above mentioned.

Partial payments to be made as follows:

First payment,

Second payment,

Third payment, etc.

The parties to these presents bind themselves, each unto the other, and in witness whereof set their hands and seals the day and year above written.

Signed, sealed, and delivered in the presence of 97

Architects generally use the form of contract which has been adopted and is recommended for general use by the American Institute of Architects and the National Association of Builders. These forms may be had of the Inland Architect Press, No. 19 Tribune Building, Chicago, and they are the most complete of any of the blanks published. Provisions are made in them for every exigency, including every point in the above agreement, as well as for additional or extra work, and the arbitration of values thereof; condemnation of materials; failure of the contractor to perform agreements; provisions for completing the work in case of such failure; times when different portions of the work are to be completed; exceptions to delays caused by strikes; unusual action of the elements, etc.; certificates from architect for payments; indemnifications against liens and claims; insurance, etc., etc.

Asbestos Cement and
Cement Dry Mortar

Both for Plastering: Walls and Ceilings.

The former to be used with sand. The latter (being already mixed with sand) requires but the addition of water.

J. B. KING & CO.,

Sole Patentees and Manufacturers, 21-24 State Street, New York, N. Y. EVIDENCE OF ITS MERITS.
Of the leading structures in the City of New York which are plastered with our *Windsor Asbestos Cement* we mention but a few, as follows:

Cornelius Vanderbilt's Mansion, Mail and Express Building,

Postal Telegraph Building, Mutual Life Insurance Building,

Continental Fire Insurance Bldg,, Mutual Reserve Life Ins. Building,

Lawyers' Title and Guarantee Bldg., The Sheldon Building,

Holland House, Bloomingdale Asylum,

American Tract Society Building, New York Life Ins. Building, etc.

As in New YORK, so in other large cities, it has been used on many of the finest buildings. Further and universal practical testimony of the great merits and appreciation of our *Windsor Cement* is that leading architects throughout the country have called for it on their best and most costly structures, while architects generally have specified it for all kinds and grades of buildings, expensive and inexpensive, as extra cost does not debar its use on even the humblest cottage. *Millions of barrels of it have been used within the last three years. Send for our complete treatise on the subject of "Needed Improvement in Plaster for Walls and Ceilings,"* and *List of Buildings* on which Windsor Cement has been used.

A Siphon-Jet Combination.

A

Sanitary
Fixture.

Has 8-inch water seal, which prevents sewer gas escaping into the building.

Everything about this closet is first-class in workmanship and finish.

Embossed closet.

Veneered tank.

Furnished in light oak, antique oak, ash, and light cherry.

Tank set on cast brass brackets, nickelplated.

Seat attachment is both neat and durable.

MANUFACTURED BY THE HAYDENVILLE MANUFACTURING CO., 73 Beekman St., New York. PLUMBERS' AND STEAM FITTERS' SUPPLIES.
These are in every respect strictly first-class Paints, composed of pure linseed oil and the highest grade of pigment.

They are combined by processes exclusively our own, and are unequaled by any in richness and permanency of color. Prepared ready for the brush in 56 Newest Shades. We are pleased to answer inquiries from all who contemplate painting their houses; to make suggestions regarding colors to be used, and to give estimate of quantity and cost of paint necessary.

SHINGLE STAINS.--Composed of pure colors and the best preservative materials known. Prepared ready for use, in twenty colors.
H. W. JOHNS MANUFACTURING CO.,
87 Maiden Lane, New York.
JERSEY CITY. CHICAGO. BOSTON. PHILADELPHIA. LONDON.
TUTTLE i BAILEY MANUFACTURING CO., MANUFACTURERS OF WARM AIR REGISTERS,
VENTILATORS, ORNA-
MENTAL SCREENS, Etc.
83 Beekman Street, NEW YORK. MAN-

UFACTURERS OF PORCELAIN LINED BATHS AND SANITARY SPECIALTIES. NEW BRIGHTON, PA.,--U. S. A. *BATH TUBS. SITZ BATH. FOOT BATH. SANITARY AND PRACTICALLY EVERLASTING. AT A MODERATE COST. Indorsed and Specified by all Leading A rchitects. The following is only one of many:*
Office Frank T. Lent, Architect,

Cranford, N. J. *Messrs. Dawes & Myler, New Brighton, Pa. Gentlemen:* The porcelain lined iron bath tub which was made by you and put in my house here two years ago is a capital thing. It shows no wear, and I could ask for no better. FRANK T. LENT.

Price, S5O.OO.

CURNISHING water heated as it flows directly from the mains. No water-back. No kitchen boiler. With this Heater the act of drawing water from any hot-water faucet in the house Automatically Turns On the Gas, which is in the same way Instantly Shut Off when the flow of water is stopped at the faucet. The Springfield Gas Machine.
The Combination Mixing Regulator.
Gas Ranges.
Gas Laundry Stoves.
j» GILBERT & BARKER MFG. CO., 82 John Street, New York. TBfE challenge anyone to show us a house where our Shingle Stain has washed off. It does not blacken; holds its color superior to paint. The greens give a beautiful effect of moss green on the roof, and the velvety effect which is regarded as highly artistic is gained by the use of these Stains. One gallon will dip about 500 shingles or cover about 125 square feet if the shingles are on the building. Write to DEXTER BROTHERS, 55 Broad Street, Boston, For Samples.
Staten Island Terra Gotta Lumber Co.
Fireproof Building Materials in Porous
Terra Gotta and Hard Tile.
ARCHITECTURAL TERRA COTTA.
ORNAMENTAL FRONT BRICKS. FIRE BRICKS.
J. EDWARD ADDICKS,) receivers ROBERT W. LYLE, JOHN V. BACOT,) ''""-Gen. Manager *Evening Address: Hotel Imperial, New York.*

Office and Factories:

Woodbridge, N. J. Insist upon having them for your BURGLAR ALARMS,
MEDICAL APPARATUS,
CALL BELLS,
GAS LIGHTERS,
ETC., ETC., ETC.

They are sure to do the work.
LAW BATTERY COMPANY, CRANFORD, NEW JERSEY. RUSSELL ft ERWIN MFG. CO.,
New Britain, Conn.
New York.
Philadelphia.
Baltimore
London.
MAKERS OF *ARTISTIC BUILDERS' HARDWARE* IN BRONZE, BRASS,
And IRON METALS.

.The Woodworks through a brass tube inserted i.'thT.p.rtuni in the earthenware, and i "thl ig".ent of fou. matcer. The s 16800 TOW 500, DRAWINGS AND SPECIFICATIONS MADE FOR ALL KINDS OF SUBURBAN BUILDINGS *ON THE BASIS OF ECONOMY ESPECIALLY.* DWELLINGS, SCHOOLS, BUSINESS BLOCKS, CLUBHOUSES, STABLES, Etc. OR the past twelve years I have made Suburban Archi tecture a special study, and during that time have designed buildings aggregating in total cost over one million dollars.

My offices at Cranford, New Jersey, are thoroughly-equipped, and I make a specialty of preparing Drawings and Specifications for all parts of the country. I have designed buildings for Maine, Massachusetts, Connecticut, New York, New Jersey, Colorado, California, Louisiana, North Carolina,.etc., and to show that my work has been successful, I insert the following extracts from clients' letters.

Lowell, Mass., March 12, 1893. Frank T. Lent, Architect: *Dear Sir:* Your drawings for our new house are all that could be desired. We are delighted with them, and owe you many thanks for your courtesies and promptness. We intend to follow your instructions in every way, and feel much pleased with the taste you have displayed. We feel assured that you will hear from Lowell again. Yours, etc., DR. BENJ. BENOIT.

Linden, N. J., June 15, 1892. Mr. F. T. Lent: *Dear Sir:* I have received the drawings and specifications for the house I propose to build here, and wish to say that in every respect I consider them the most complete and perfect of any I have ever seen.

Yours truly, OSCAR GESSNER, D. D.

These letters are especially valuable, because in the case of Dr. Benoit the work was all perfected by means of correspondence. I have never seen Dr. Benoit. The second letter is from a gentleman of broad building experience— he having built a number of houses. *Correspondence solicited.* FRANK T. LENT, *Suburban Arclritetl, Cranford, New Jersey.*

Lane's Patent Steel Barn Door Hanger, ANTI-FRICTION. MOST COMPLETE IN CONSTRUCTION.

MATERIAL THE BEST. NO BREAKAGE.

Ease of Movement. Always in Order.

Lane's Patent Noiseless Steel Parlor Door Hanger.

Hanger is made of steel throughout, including wheel, except solid interior leather tread, causing to roll noiselessly.

Single Steel Track instead of Double Wood Rail.

Ask you Hardware Dealer, and send for Circular. Manufactured by l.ANE BROTHERS, Poughkeepsie, N. Y.

has a soft, velvety color effect, which lasts as long as the best paint, and is much superior in appearance. Creosote Stains cost 50 per cent, less than paint to buy, and save fully one-half the time and labor in application.

"Wood treated with (Creosote) is not subject to dry rot Or Other decay."— *Century Dictionary.*

A scientific insulator and deafener, which makes its own dead-air spaces. Actual tests prove that one layer is better than six of rosin-sized paper. *It is cheaper to build sound and cold-proof houses than to regret not doing so.*

Quilt and Stain samples, with circulars and color studies,
sent on request.
SAMUEL CABOT, Sole Manufacturer, BOSTON, MASS.

Is the manufacturing of Heating and Cooking Apparatus. Our experience of

nearly fifty years is at your service. If interested, and you will indicate the method of heating desired, we will send you illustrated catalogue.

We Manufacture 195 and 197 Lake Street, CHICAGO.
307 and 209 Water Street, NEW YORK.
DO YOU USE WflTER? DO YOU WANT IT EVERY DflY?

Only the best pump will meet this want. The best ones are the
Rider and Ericsson Hot-Air Pumps.

Is a record of twenty years proof enough? They are not the "cheapest/ The best of anything is never cheapest in first cost. But you do not buy pumps every day, and in the " long run" the lowest-priced things are not always the cheapest. Any boy can run our engines, and under all circumstances they are absolutely safe. If interested, send for catalogue lt B.2,M and state conditions under which your pump will have to work.
RIDER ENGINE CO., 86 Lake St., Chicago. 37 Dey St., New York.

To be of pure stock and perfect braid, and it may be identified at sight by its distinctive mark—the spot. If your dealer doesn't keep it, send to SAMSON CORDAGE WORKS, Boston, Mass. YOU ARE RESPONSIBLE AS AN ARCHITECT OR BUILDER

For the strength and character of your work. The Best made and
Best known Cement is the
"F. O. Norton" Brand

Adopted by leading Architects and Builders.
OFFICE: 92 Broadway, New York City.

We are the only makers of Porcelain-lined baths who manufacture but one quality and guarantee every tub turned out.

When you find S. M. Co. on the bottom of a bath tub, there is no risk.
SEND FOR CATALOGUE. STANDARD MANUFACTURING CO., PITTSBURGH, PA. Samples may *be seen* at
No. 8 East 42d St., N. Y.
WHEELER'S PATENT WOOD FILLER.

For beauty of finish and durability no wood should be naturally finished without first filling the pores with this article. Insist on having the genuine only. See that our name as manufacturers

Lightning Source UK Ltd.
Milton Keynes UK
UKOW06f1015160913

217275UK00002B/176/P